Traveling in a Dream
& Other Stories

Kim Lan Tran

NEW CENTURY FORUM

Hatgåña   Chicago

EDITOR'S NOTE

Kim Lan and I have been the best of friends for half a century. We were roommates in college at Emmanuel in Boston. 'Golden Orchid', her Vietnamese name, evokes the image of a delicate, beautiful, rare flower that gives pleasure and delight to those who catch a glimpse. Lan's stories evoke the same image and reactions. To the reader, her ability to draw the unsuspecting passerby into intense moments of human interaction, clearly puts her in the rank of great storytellers. It has been my honor and pleasure to work with her on this book project. Lan and I have relished our friendship and conversations about all kinds of subjects through the years we have known each other. The intimacy of stepping into a friend's experience through reflection and recollection is binding and has added depth to my profound respect for her talent.

The graphic of the Vietnamese drum is a symbol of the endurance and longevity of the Vietnamese ancient culture. Here, it is a symbol of the endurance of lived experience through written stories.

Laura M. Torres Souder, Ph.D.
Author, *Daughters of the Island*

TRAVELING IN A DREAM & OTHER STORIES.

ACKNOWLEDGMENTS

My thanks go to my fellow writers of OLLI (Osher Lifelong Learning Institute) at University of Massachusetts, Boston for their support and comments. In particular, I would like to thank Laura M. Torres Souder, Michael H. Cunningham, and Hugh Stringer for reading, encouragement, and editing the manuscript of *Traveling in A Dream.*

CONTENTS

Traveling in a Dream

& Other Stories

A STONE OF GOLD

Many times, in my life I wish for a miracle that would turn something unworthy into a valuable one, just like a small piece of dirty stone in my palm once suddenly turned to gold.

I was about eight years old then, living with my aunt and her family in Saigon city during one of the wars in Viet Nam. My parents had sent me to be under her care for my safety. I was, fortunately, safe from the fighting, the shooting or the bombing, but I did not feel safe in her home.

I was on guard all the time. I had to watch my every movement, and any noise I made for fear of being reprimanded, cursed, or punished in various means: whipping, humiliating, being made to eat something I craved for to vomit. I wept as I forced my throat to swallow piece by piece of ripened mangoes. To this day, the sight of orange mango still repulses me. I said I had to watch my movements because, if I walked fast I was called a horse; and, if I moved slowly my name would be a turtle.

I had chronic sinus. I restrained myself from blowing my nose by swallowing my mucus. This irritated my throat and made me cough. During the night, I buried my head beneath the blanket and padded a pillow on top of it to muffle my sneezes or coughs. "Stop coughing. No more noise from you. You hear me, devil?"" I still hear the echo of my aunt's shrill voice at times. I constantly worried about my "wrong doings" and punishments.

After school, I did all sorts of chores: babysitting, taking care of any dirty jobs and doing errands. The day my aunt sent me to the drying cleaner to pick up here husband's pants was the most unforgettable day in my childhood. I came home from the cleaner and handed her the pants in a nylon bag. She took the pants out of the bag and immediately rolled here big round fish-like eyes and glared at me. "One pair is missing. Go back to the shop and tell the owner. You're good for nothing. Better feeding the dog than feeding you." She snarled. I hurried back to the shop, which was quite a distance from home. I was sweating, panting, and trembling all over under the burning sun. My legs carried me faster than my normal pace. Stammering in my weak voice I told the shop owner what had happened. He shook his head telling me it was not true. He had had given me three pairs of pants instead of two.

I did not go straight home. I took refuge in a huge cement culvert placed away from the sidewalk. I sat there for a while, trying to figure out what to do next. A piece of stone covered with dirt caught my eyes. I cleaned it and held it tightly in my hand. I closed my eyes and silently asked the Superior to turn that piece of stone into a piece of gold. I needed the money to buy another pair of pants. I held my breath for a while and opened my fist. Nothing had changed. There was no stone of gold. With the black stone in my hand I walked and walked, crossed one street after another. Running through the traffic, I passed heaps and heaps of pungent and muddy trash dumps. I found myself in the midst of an unsafe section of the town. The fear of not knowing what lay ahead was engulfing me, pushing me forward like a fierce wind. My legs kept moving faster and faster. I ended up at the door of a shack, the home of my aunt's cook. She let me stay for the night.

That night I sneezed and coughed freely like anyone else. I knew I would have to face my aunt's stormy anger the next day. There would be no way to avoid it. Nevertheless, my heart was somewhat lighter with the thought that I was ready to take the blow for I had the cook's empathy.

***

Years later I worked as a clinician in America, helping my clients to understand themselves and others, I occasionally thought about my aunt's ill treatment and I came to realize that I happened to be an escape goat in her home. I had heard she was a good mother and a devoted wife but I also heard some whispering among relatives, and talking behind her back from her neighbors. They said she endured the silence of secrets in her marriage and did not feel good about herself. I really don't know how much her self-esteem and self-image affected her personality and how bad her marriage was. I only knew for a fact that she had changed in her old age. She was emotional needy and required a lot of attention from those who treated her with empathy.

MY CRYING

I didn't cry often, but when I cried, I sobbed. When I sobbed, I didn't shed a lot of tears. I just gasped.

As a teen-ager living away from my parents during the French war in Vietnam I served those who took me in. I looked after their children. I had a nephew who cried consistently whenever his parents went out. He cried with real tears and determination. I did different things to calm him down. I coaxed him, gave him candy, and promised to buy toys. I took him to a playground and pointed at the boys giggling while they were at play to distract him from his painful separation from his mother. I let him rest on my chest and gently tapped on his back to comfort him. He would not stop crying.

Feeling his anguish, I started crying. I cried louder than he did. If anyone looked into my heart they would see that I cried for my lot, which could be loneliness, homesickness, helplessness, frustration, or a profound need of love and attention. Anyway, my crying worked. My nephew was totally surprised by the hiccup sound coming out of his aunt's throat. He jerked his head, looked at me with curiosity and stopped crying.

In a dormitory of an American college I made a few good friends who were on scholarships from different parts of the world. Each one had a history of heartbreak. One day a dear friend of mine ran to me to tell me her fresh wound of another failed romance. We held each other tightly. She cried and cried and I sobbed and sobbed. I sobbed hard and long. I felt her arms gradually leaving my shoulders. Then she stopped crying. She looked away and sniffled. Thinking back, I realized I cried double. I cried for my friend's lost love and for mine, too.

Part of my job as a school psychologist was to counsel children with emotional issues. Once I asked a sixth grader to draw a picture of a human figure. He drew a man standing behind iron bars. In tears, he said, "My father is in jail."

Although his story was not uncommon to me I could not help holding back my tears. He took a piece of tissue out of his pocket and gave it to me. Years later I bumped into him in a high school. We stunned for a moment finding word to say to each other. I was happy to see a tall youngster wearing a bright smile. He then quickly said as pointing at his flying afro hair, "Ms. Tran, it's just a bad hair day. Don't worry, everything else is okay."

I have lost some of my loved ones. I felt numbed by my grief until I received heartfelt condolences from relatives. Their kind words triggered my sorrow, guilt, and repressed feelings. I regretted that I was not much of a daughter or a sister. I did not take care of them the way I have wished because life in a strange land was just too hard for me.

If someone happened to pass by my apartment during my mourning time, he would halt his steps, discreetly listen to my convulsive weep, and walk away with a heavy heart.

SAFE REVENGE

She is an English lady, a tourist. She ordered roasted lamb chops and tea.

"I'd like my tea now." She said.

I disappeared for a little while and brought tea to her. As I turned my back heading to the kitchen, she called after me, pointing at the cup of tea and asked, "Is this tea?"

"Yes, Madam, it's tea." I answered.

"Tell your manager this is not tea."

"Yes, Madam."

I walked towards the manager, who stood at the front door greeting the customers and said to him, "Mr. G., the lady over there said what we served was not tea."

"Let me take care of that," he said calmly.

"I returned to her table with a plate of steaming lamb chops that smelled exotic spices and garnished with green parsley, an orange slice, and something red. Nice!

The lady looked at the plate and at me. Then she asked, "Where's the mint sauce?"

"What sauce, Madam?

"I don't eat lamb without mint sauce," she explained.

"I'll be right back, Madam."

"Mint sauce!" I said to myself. "What on earth is it? Never heard of it before. How am I supposed to know what it is? Never had lamb chops in my life. Oh God! This is difficult. Yesterday someone ordered Bloody Mary, and another wanted Manhattan on the rocks. I asked the bartender why people wanted blood and rocks in their drinks. He had a good laugh and told me it was the name of the drink and rocks were ice cubes. "You have a lot to learn, baby. Take it easy. If someone bothers you, let me know." He said.

I thanked him, smiled, and walked away. He sent his words after me, "Make sure you leave that smile here in America when you go back to Vietnam, ok, Babe."

I asked one of the waitresses where the mint sauce was. She told me to check with the cook. We were frantic but manage to find some mint sauce at last. When I brought out the sauce the food was not warm enough. The lady asked me to warm it up. I took the plate, went to the kitchen, heated it up, and brought it back to her. She began to cut the meat into small pieces, gracefully eating one by one. As she was leaving she gave me a twenty=dollar bill, telling me that it wasn't my fault for all the trouble. She was surprised that a prestigious restaurant in the heart of Boston did not know how to serve lamb chops.

Twenty years later I was in London for a one-day trip, sitting in the Hop-On Hop-Off sightseeing bus watching people from the countries that border England rushing to London for a few big sale days. I tried to be as observant as possible. The bus passed Buckingham Palace. I could not believe my eyes when seeing the real guards in their bright uniforms walk back and forth. Then my mind ran wild with comments: "Modernization. The gothic buildings. The luxurious department stores. The Queen ... and Shakespeare. A great combination! I was exuberant. I had the nerve to major in English literature but knew very little about England. I cried over Shakespeare's masterpieces not because his stories were touching but because I could not understand his English. I remembered our English professor, a nun, told us to leave the auditorium during her lecture on Byron, an English poet, if we thought we did not belong there. I felt I did not belong there but I stayed.

When the bus stopped at Waterloo Station I got off, stepped into a crowded restaurant. I ordered lamb chops. Looking at the plate I asked the waiter, "Where's the mint sauce?" He gave me a surprised look. I guessed nobody cared for mint sauce anymore. Right at that moment I found myself being difficult.

"I can't eat lamb without mint sauce." I said, shaking my head.

From where I sat I saw the waiter mix something together. He poured the mixture it a small cup and brought it to me. The sauce smelled mint all right, but it had a strange taste, not like the real jelly mint sauce that I had become accustomed to over the years. I gave the waiter a ten-dollar bill, saving the shillings for the rest of the day. He gave me another surprised look, probably because I did not look rich. I wasn't.

In one of the busy streets I stopped an elder in his elegant suit to ask for directions. He drew a map of my way, clearly and wholeheartedly. When I said thank you to him he responded in a deep and warm voice, a voice that has been comforting me whenever I hear it in my head: "You're welcome, my lo

MY INNER WILDNESS

I have never thought of myself as being wild. Wildness to me is anything relating to being unconventional, risky, scary, lonely, and unrealistic. However, circumstances did make me wild.

I grew up in a culture that shaped a female to be obedient as a child and submissive as a woman. There was no room for opposition to adults, particularly to men. I became a product of their creation. I was not supposed to make eye contact when talking, or to voice my opinion for some decision that was against my will such as getting married to a mismatched mate. Confucius teaching for my so-called the weak gender was ingrained in our ancestors' minds: "When living at home a woman must obey her father. When married, listen to her husband, and after her husband died, follow her son's instruction." In reflection on my 'unacceptable' behaviors to my people I realized that I have been wild. Several times in my life I took risk, swimming against the stream to survive or to fulfill my needs.

My family expected me to learn the trade of a seamstress. But I dreamed of a teaching job. One of my teachers was my role model. She was knowledgeable, understanding, and caring. I wanted to follow her steps and also to please my parents. I learned how to sew during daytime and attended evening classes for the academics. After many years of hard work on my part and much doubt for my success from my loved ones, I got a scholarship from Emmanuel college in Boston, Massachusetts, and became a teacher.

Many of us are victims of wars or political ideology. I accidently fell into that category. I used to live in South Vietnam. After North Vietnam won what was known as the American war in 1975, the Southerners who had something to do with the American ally were not trusted by the new regime under the communist rulers. I escaped from my country out of fear, the fear of being accused as a traitor for having been educated in the United States.

Living in a foreign country with little money and a child I was scared and lonely. I fought my way up with caution and determination. I had no choice but to be the sole master of my decision making. My husband passed away years ago.

My son now is a man. He has his own dreams and I have mine. Fortunately, he has no intention making me follow his direction and I would not let him do so anyway. I have had a plan for the last years of my life. I quitted a job with good pay to avoid harmful stress and to save time for pursuing my love of the arts and to do volunteer work. I have taken courses in writing, music, and drawing. I give free language lessons. To my folks, I am unrealistic for not making money when I still can. To me, doing something to fulfill my needs is necessary and rewarding.

My inner wildness, thus, is just against adversities in order to survive. The wildness in me does not include doing something harmful to others such as hurting my

20

family name or my sanity. Part of me is still the product of a culture that keeps a woman in line for her safety. Men or the strong gender is certainly honorable to those who need protection. I am one of them.

TRAVELING IN A DREAM

The classroom. The students. The teacher. In early fall, the classroom is airy with windows wide open. The wind lurks from the trees, gently sweeping over the green grass, rushing through the windows, lifting the students' spirits. On winter days, a large white blanket of snow covers the playground. The windows are tightly closed.

It was then during one cold day the younger students shrank in their warm clothes but some older and bigger ones tried to be cool, wearing sleeveless shirts to show off their muscles. Their lips turned pale. Their bodies shook slightly.

The teacher reminded the whole class, "This is New England. America is not like our country, Vietnam, where the weather is warm all year round. You have to make an effort to wear warm clothes, and don't forget your scarves and hats.

"Oh! Not cold at all." One of the boys said out loud, "I've been through worse. A boat person like me survived the storm and the freezing for months in the middle of the ocean."

Another voice interjected, "Oh please, Great grandfather! Don't even try to boast. What cow head borrowed my coat yesterday?"

The teacher raised her voice to a higher note, "You have to listen to me. If you get sick you'll miss classes, and besides, it's boring to stay home for days. Do you understand?"

"Already understood. We heard you. Go ahead and teach. I'm tired of your advice."

The teacher raised her voice a note higher, "Nhuận, watch your language. Have you forgotten what you have been taught?"

Nhuận brazenly challenge the teacher, "Come on teacher, I lost it a long time. Actually, nobody taught me anything. You're the only one who makes me the way I am."

The teacher changed her tone of voice to an octave lower, trying to repress her anger and said, "Nhuận! You want me to send you to the principal's office?"

"I don't care. I'll go. Don't be bossy just because you're a teacher!"

He walked out of the classroom without waiting for an order. The teacher called after him, "Come back to get the permission slip!"

"Eh! Cow Head, you forgot permission slip? Watch out for the cops. They're out there in the hallway," one of his classmates, Sam, chimed in. And to the teacher, he said, "Teacher, teacher, Nhuận made trouble because he wants to be suspended. He wants go to Chinatown to watch porn movies."

Nhuận returned to the class, snatched the permission slip from the teacher's hand, raising his fist and threatening Sam, "I'll beat the hell out of your mother. What do you know, kiddo?"

The teacher yelled, "Quiet! No more talking!"

Her angry, loud voice startled the students. No sounds were heard for a while. She distributed work and flopped into the chair, releasing a deep sigh, feeling dejected by Nhuận's absence. Suddenly the sound 'pop, pop' of bubble gum blowing disturbed the silence. The teacher rose, glanced around, and asked, "Who's chewing gum?"

"Eh! Who is it? Better confess or else you'll be in deep trouble if the teacher finds out." One of the class clown attempted to be helpful.

The teacher spotted a girl wearing bright red lipstick, dark blue mascara, and a hairstyle that gave the impression that somebody had played a joke on her. She signaled the girl to go to the wastebasket. The girl reluctantly stood up, continued to gnaw a piece of gum between her front teeth, smiling widely.

Hoan could not help making his comments, "This teacher is dangerous. Can't believe it, she sees everything up there!"

The teacher announced, "You have only twenty minutes. Stop talking and concentrate on your work!"

Another voice was heard loud and clear, "Damn it! American language is so difficult. I forgot all what I studied last night."

The students roared with laughter. The teacher suppressed hers, raising her voice, "Be quiet! If you need to say something, raise your hand."

"Teacher, I have a question. How come the Americans are very impolite? They address their grandparents and grandchildren using only the word 'YOU.' It's confusing, very difficult to tell who's older."

The teacher did not get a chance to answer what was asked when out of the blue a conversation among three students interrupted,

"Give me back my pencil, Devil!"

"Fat Elephant, since when did I take your pencil?"

"Did I swallow all your grandfather's wealth to be fat?"

"Eh, Fat Hue, where did you sell fish in Vietnam? I can't stand a girl who talks mean and vulgar."

The teacher interfered, "Tam, don't call you friend names. Get rid of the words 'fat', 'crossed eyes', 'shorty', and so on. One only hears a name calling once and might feel sad the rest of his or her life."

The word 'sad' seemed to have a strong effect on the students. The whole class silently did their work, except one boy, who rested his head on his desk. The teacher came to his side, feeling his forehead. She whispered in his ear, "Mạnh, are you okay? You want to step out to tell me what happened."

"I know, I know what happened to him. Broken heart. Last night he was drunk, vomiting all over. He said he hated life and his betrayed lover.' Giỏi said.

Mạnh tried to pull himself together, yelling at Giỏi, "Shut your mouth, VC. I'll break your neck when we get home. Beast, I hate your father's race."

Phong interfered to explain the relationship between Mạnh and Giỏi, "He's not a Vietnamese Communist. He is Korean. It's the truth, teacher. The younger brother has Korean blood and the older one has French blood. Don't you see he looks more handsome than those who have American blood?"

Manh turned around retorted, "Who said I had French blood. My mother has. I officially Amerasian."

The teacher announced, "When you finish your work, leave it on my desk. I need to talk to Mạnh."

Outside the classroom Mạnh leaned against the wall, appearing depressed.

The teacher asked, "Are you okay?"

"Nothing."

"You are only fourteen. "Stop drinking alcohol. It's bad for your health. Can you tell me what bothers you?"

"Nothing. Yến stopped talking to me. I drank to forget her."

"Let me ask her why," I said, "Maybe something troubled her. You made yourself sick before you find out the real reason behind her way of treating you. Review your lessons. I'll give you another chance to make up your work."

"Thank you, teacher."

Manh dragged himself into the classroom, looking like a defeated soldier. Nhi made her know-it-all comment, "Hey, everyone, look at Mạnh's face. It's the look of a person who lost his rice ration!" Ngô jumped out of his

26

seat, yelling at Nhi, "Shut up! Idiot! No rice ration in this country. Buy as much rice as you want supermarkets."

The tallest boy in the class named Tịnh, stretching his long arms, yawning, and talked to himself, "Man, what a strange country! There is plenty of rice and meat. You can eat until you throat turns inside out, and yet it's a sad, sad country. I'd rather go back home, tending my paddy. It's more fun."

Hearing the giggles, he said, "Make fun of me if you wish. You guys know nothing. I was the best farmer there. I planted rice very well."

One boy exclaimed, "Come on. Don't show off. I bet I did it better than you."

Tâm, who had been quiet for a while, suddenly stood up, talking to the whole class, "Who doesn't know how to work the rice fields? Let me show you." Then he began to bend down, pretending to make the movements of a farmer in action. He did it with rhythm and grace like a dancer. The teacher watched him in awe. She had not ever seen him so lively and happy. She turned her back to the class, trying to hide her tears, feeling sorry for the children who longed for their homeland.

Giỏi would not miss such a fun opportunity. He rolled on the floor, laughing whole-heartedly.

The bell rang. Classes were over. The teacher left the classroom, standing in the hallway to watch the students go to their different classes. Students of all races came out from classrooms on both sides of the hallway. Some looked sleepy carrying their heavy steps. Others showed

27

themselves full of energy, attempting to rush ahead, pushing and cutting lines. The teacher moved away from the crowd standing at the bottom of the stairway, chanting like a Chinese waiter selling noodle soup, "Single line on the right!"

A student came close to her, whispering, "I don't like to stay in a single line and I am allergic to the word RIGHT."

Pretending not to hear what he said, the teacher repeated the same line in her language to the Vietnamese students, "Đi hàng một bên phải."

From upstairs, students rushed down. They jumped two or three steps at a time. Their shoelaces flapped along their way. It was like a battalion passing by, leaving a strip of dust flying in the sunbeam coming from the window above. The teacher held her breath avoiding the smell of dust mixed with sweat, deodorant, and hair spray. She remained at her place, waiting until the rest of the students to settle into their classrooms.

The noise soon died down, but some students still lingered, trying to avoid boring lessons a little longer. A girl with hair braids like snakes curving, approached. Her heavy breasts shook gently at each of her steps. Her big eyes gazed into a void. She seemed unaffected by her surroundings. It was said she had a baby. She probably did not have a good night sleep. Statistics say every two minutes there is a teen-age girl giving birth to a child. America is known as a country that has a high number of adolescent abortions.

The teacher was deep in her thoughts when she heard her name called by a colleague, Bill. He said, "Linh, Linh. Come here, I want to ask you something."

Linh stepped closer to Bill. He showed her a piece of paper he took it off from the back of a student's shirt, and asked Linh what the writing meant. "Please feel free to punch. No need to be polite," Linh translated.

Bill laughed and said, "Vietnamese students have manners even in fights! You have a free period? Please teach my class. I can't stand them anymore."

Linh looked into Bill's class. Heads with straight hair, curly hair, black, blond, and red hair were moving up and down, turning left and right to avoid paper balls flying from all directions. She comforted her colleague, "In my country there is a saying, 'Satan comes first, ghost comes second and student comes third.' "What? What did you say?" Bill exclaimed, "In this country student comes first. Satan and ghost are last!"

Bill threw a quick look at his class and mumbled, "It has been thirty years! It's too late to change a career. "Should have become a dentist. No, no. You get more money but still work with children. A pilot. Yes. A pilot, flying up in the sky, leaving this earth."

Linh returned to her class. She looked at the empty desks, and thought of Nhuận. He was tall and skinny with hair touching his eyes, which blinked constantly due to poor vision. He seemed to care for attending to trends more than learning. Then she thought of other troubled students and said to herself, "And yet the American colleagues think I'm lucky to have Vietnamese students!" A stern look from her would be enough to correct her students' misbehavior. That belonged to the past when she used to teach English in schools and tutor students in their homes to get them ready for going abroad. With a Bachelor's degree from the United States and a Bostonian accent she was treated with honor and showered with gifts. It was different now. After a couple of years in America many Vietnamese children adopted excellent accents. They would not let go any mistake she made when mispronouncing a word.

She walked around the class, picturing each face that she had had the opportunity to know them for several years. She silently said to herself, "This is Đức's seat. He is unable to sit still for five minutes. After many times telling him to control his fidgety in vain, she said to him, "It's very difficult to teach you, Đức."

He quickly responded, "Give me a hundred dollars, you can teach me easily. I only care for money."

Đức considered a classroom an open market. He asked for an "A" in advance and swore on his life he would study later.

The desk on the left was Nhâm's seat. His motto: "Hit back when being attacked. Forbearing insult is humiliation." was often repeated by his classmates. Nobody had heard from him for months. His friends said he traveled far to protect the weak!

The two desks in the back of the class were Ngôn's resting place. He could not keep awake. He said he was too tired from working night shifts. Kiên cared a lot for Ngôn. He begged the teacher to let his friend sleep.

Thinking of Kiên she remembered his strong arms and big hands from years of pulling fishnets. He frequently forgot his pencils. After a while Linh found out that he was too clumsy to hold small objects. The last time Linh saw him he looked well groomed, saying his grades started to improve when he was suddenly 'hit hard with love.' "Love is very strong, teacher. A muscular one like me can still get knocked out really bad."

The other students were those who matured early. Not only did they succeed academically, but also quickly learned to adapt to the host country. On newspapers, honored students named Tran or Nguyen had become as familiar as Smith and Brown. Being impressed with their achievements, their American teachers thought highly of all Vietnamese.

Linh settled herself in her chair. She looked through the window, contemplating the church behind the bare tall trees, and asking herself whether there was peace inside the cathedral.

Hearing a knock on the door she turned to say hello to Jeff, her co-worker. Jeff asked her, "You're dreaming again? Watch out! Romantic thoughts could kill you easily."

"Would not dare. I know my limitations. I had a hard time controlling the class today. They went wild. I am a bit down, letting my mind wander."

"My class was the same. Probably because of the full moon or too much sugar intake. It is just a daily matter. Don't torture yourself. Students come and go. Do you want to feel bad all your career life? I've told you, only desperate people like us meet right here, choosing this job."

"That's not true. I've seen you teach with passion, lecturing like someone in a trance."

Jeff laughed mirthfully, explaining, "Sometimes I have an illusion that God sent me to earth to change the destiny of mankind. You want to go to the cafeteria?"

"No, thank you. I'm on duty. It's my turn to guard this area. You know Jeff, in my country the job of a teacher is teaching, nothing else. Here we also do the work of a nurse, a secretary, and a policeman. We have to take care of our students' hygiene, know their life history, and make sure there are no dangerous weapons or drugs in schools."

"Yeah. Yeah. This educational system surely needs a reform. Also, the more social values loosen, the harder we work. You came here to share our fate."

The bell rang. Classes were over. Jeff waved his hand good bye, trying to comfort Linh, "Cheer up! Today is Friday and also payday. Such a privilege! What else do you want?"

Linh smiled and hastily stepped out to the corridor. Even one minute delayed could be trouble. An unexpected kiss from a boy to a girl, or a fall caused by a kick for a tease was enough to start a big fight.

Though Linh was busy interfering with complaints from different parties she could not help the refrains from upstairs: "Brian, get rid of your gums." "Natasha, are you fifteen or sixteen years old? Why do you still suck your thumb?" "Fernando, leave the locker alone. Why do you have to kick it?" "Shirley, kiss your desk goodbye. Didn't you hear the bell ring? Did you guys understand what I said? Single line means one head behind another. I speak plain English, no other languages. Why can't you understand?"

As Linh was entering her classroom she heard her name announcing on the loud speaker. She asked Bill to help watching her class and hurried to the school office. The principal pointed at a boy standing in the corner and said to her, "This is Tôn. He refuses to go to school. His foster parents said he needs a bilingual program and especially a warm hand of someone from his homeland. They don't speak Vietnamese."

'A warm hand of someone from his homeland' touched Linh's weak point. Without hesitating she put her hand on Tôn's shoulder. He pushed her away and gave her a hard kick on her leg. Linh staggered. She tried to compose herself and gently said to him, "I'm a teacher here. You want to come to my class? It may be fun. There are many boys your age."

"I already said I don't want to be in school. Why do people keep forcing me?" He wailed as he was kicking the wall.

Shocked by the principal's angry voice commanding him to stop kicking Tôn grasped the lock on the desk and attempted to throw it at him. The principal quickly

33

restrained him and held him down on the floor. Tôn wiggled his body, screaming, and spitting. The principal wiped the saliva on his face and pasted it on Tôn's. Linh kneeled down, trying to calm both of them in two languages. "Don't worry. I'm calm." The principal said in his trembling voice. "You tell him if he does not stop making noise I'll call the police."

Hearing the word "police" the boy subdued. He called Linh for help, "Auntie, auntie, tell him to let go my arms. He is killing me!"

Linh interpreted what Tôn said. The principal released his grip. Tôn crawled to the corner or the room, whimpering.

Later Linh learned that Tôn had followed some soldiers escaping from Vietnam by boat. He had a rough life in the refugee camp, drinking, selling sex, and stealing. He was twelve years old on paper but he looked much older than his age with a stern expression and a stooped stature. On his bony arm were two tattooed letters "T.T," the first letter stands for youth, love, money, crime, imprison, and suicide in Vietnamese language. (Tình, tiền, tù, tội, tự tử) Stepping on this land he became a challenge for his guardian's compassion, painful experience for the educators, and an unbearable burden for the social workers. Other children named him "The Monkey That Raises Hell in Schools." (Tôn Ngộ Không Đại Náo Học Đường.)

One day he could not be found anywhere.

***

Snow scattered incessantly. Linh was having a fever. She slowly walked toward the bus stop across the street. A lanky figure with head down, puffing a cigarette was sitting on a bench alone. As she was coming closer, Linh recognized the youth.

"Hello, Nhuận. Why didn't you go to school today?"

"I was suspended for 3 days."

"What did you do?"

"Bothered the teacher for fun. Why aren't you teaching?"

"I'm going to see a doctor. I'm not feeling well."

Silence.

"Why didn't you stay home, Nhuận? You don't dress warm enough."

Nhuận smiled sadly and answered,

"Stay home to get beaten by my uncle? No way."

"What about your parents?"

"The old man died in Vietnam. The woman was gone forever a few months ago, here, in this country."

Silence.

"If you wish I'll make time to tutor you."

"No. It's a waste of my effort."

In the bus the two of them sat next to each other. Linh wanted to say something to make her student feel better but her body burned with fever, and Nhuận kept his thoughts to himself. After a while she asked him, "Where're you going now?"

"Don't know."

Linh got off the bus, pulling up the collar of her coat, letting her tears drip.

***

Recovering from the flu Linh felt more alive than ever. On her sick bed, she had time to think of her students' misfortunes and wanted to do something more helpful than just crying and feeling sorry for them. She tried to reach them in various ways, patiently waiting for them to learn each small step. She neither expected too much of them nor forgot to praise any minimal success. Their inappropriate language, which used to bother her ears, like hearing the sound of a bullet, was ignored. She waited for them to learn better ways of expressing themselves.

She reminded them who they really were and what they should do to survive and to gain respect in the host country. Her happiest moments were when Thanh tried to control his stutter, volunteering to recite the poem entitled "The Hour of History" by D.V.C.

"... I'm sure after the turbulent change
The Vietnamese continues to be the greatest men
I believe no one can put an end
The heroes and heroines born in our land."

She remembered when Thanh stopped reciting the poem, Xuan raised her hand to request,

"Please, teacher, give us more poem to learn by heart. Why did I have goose bumps when listening to it?"

It was the first time after ten years of teaching Linh actually felt proud of her job. She no longer missed the instant complements and the full-arm bouquets her students back home gave her at the end of each semester. Now she did not get tired of watching the bright eyes and the smiles on the faces of those who went in and out of her classroom. She practiced not to humiliate them, avoiding using the words 'stupid' or 'unteachable.' Her students also challenged her less. Giỏi did not swear as freely as he used to. When knowing his lessons well he would jump up and down, pulling Linh's sleeve and say, "Hey, teacher, I did not watch Kung Fu movies last night. I did my homework. Give me more work today. Studying is addictive."

Đức stopped negotiating for grades. He got his first A and treasured it. Mạnh made the dean's list. He told his classmates Yến belonged to history. He won the hearts of other girls easily. As for Yến, she started and ended Mạnh's fist pages of love story by a shy smile hidden behind her shining black hair.

***

At the end of the school year the children were getting ready to go on stage to receive their diplomas, graduating from eighth grade. Tâm said to the whole class, "Hey, everybody, take pictures of you in cap and gown and send them to Vietnam to impress your folks. An idiot like me also graduated after a few years studying in America!"

Nhi used her know-it-all tone again, "Yeah. Our people think there are miracles here. They simply don't know you guys are promoted to a higher grade because of your age! They don't even know you only learn bad language!"

Tâm retorted, "Mind you on business! Just because you do well in school you think you have the right to look down on us. If only I had come here two years before you, I would have been a good student, too."

Linh interrupted the argument, asking Nhuận why he did not have his gown on yet. He answered abruptly, "I burned the damn gown when ironing it!"

Hải sent Linh a wink and whispered, "He lied to you, teacher. He told me he felt ashamed to wear the gown because he did badly in school.

***

Summer vacation. The students had left two days ago, the teacher alone was busy tiding her classroom. The sunlight shined on her students' "masterpieces" hanging on the walls. The painting entitled *Children of the Dragon and Grandchildren of the Fairies* done by Nghĩa not only showed the lovely faces coming out from one hundred eggs as the legend said, but also showed their feet above the ground. "What omen is this? Does that mean we are at all not grounded?" Linh asked herself. The wind rushed through the window, blowing away the paper written by an attractive student named Tơ. Linh picked it up and saved it. Tơ's nice handwriting touched her heart. She sighed, thinking of the girl, who was bearing the child of her step-father.

Linh was going to put her students' journals in her bag and go home, but there were a couple of hours left before she could leave the school. She sat down and read over and over some of the noticeable lines:

"Dear teacher, my parents said they sacrificed their lives to give me an education. But we are new here. We do not have a car. I have to wait for buses and subway in the cold weather. My English is poor. Everything is too difficult. Please, teacher, don't be mad at me. Your student. Hoa."

"...Dear teacher, I had to look after my sister. She did not stop crying. When she did I began to do my homework, but my eyelids were really heavy. I could not open my eyes. We have a big family. Too many chores for me. I have bruises all over my body because my father beat me. He asked me why I didn't die. My brother does nothing to help out in the house and yet he is allowed to go out for fun? Teacher, Why so? Your student: Hiền."

"...I will become a hero. Then I have a lot of money. I go to Africa to bring the children here in America to learn English so they get good job. Good bye, teacher. Quốc Nguyễn."

"...Dear teacher, in the countryside where I used to live the moon shone everywhere. In this country, the moon is hard to see. Too many tall buildings. I remember on the moon nights my family enjoyed grilled fish in our front yard. It was so much fun living in Viet Nam. In America nothing else is fun but going to school. Đạt Huỳnh."

"... I *happy* to go *schol* again. My *old* big and my *min smal* I very much not *undrestan*. 12 year old I work take care my family. 17 year old I study take care me. I drive the boat bring 21 person to *iland* safe. I do my duty. *Finis my story life.* Bảo Trần"

"...Last night in my dream I went back to Viet Nam I was rich. I was 21 years old. I flew there giving dollars, gold, and diamonds to people. Then the alarm clock rang for me to get up to go to school. It was frustrated that I had not finish distributing my money to everybody. Thúy."

"... On the boat I saw two men threw my mother into the ocean. I did not talk for days. I did not eat. When I woke up I saw myself living on an island. Now I am here. I travelled from one country to another in a dream. The kids name me 'Mute Hoà' but I am not mad at them. I like school, teacher. Hoà Lê."

"...Dear teacher, yesterday I *received* a letter from my mother. She told my father not to drink too much. My father went out and did not get home till late. He was drunk. He told me not to think that he did not listen to my mother. He drank because he missed her so much. That means he still listens to her. Then we cried together. I often see my mother in my dreams. But it is really strange, teacher. Every time I reached out to touch my mother I suddenly woke up. Phong."

Linh straightened out each journal and put them away. Looking at the empty chairs, her heart was filled with tenderness and admiration for her students. She immediately took out her memo book and responded to their writing:

"My dear students, I'm struggling to get out my idealistic foolishness and my unreachable dreams to be more than ready than ever to hold your hands. I have come close to you and seen your hands, which, there was a time, swiftly threw the fishnets or skillfully cared for the rice plants. Yet, those hands became clumsy in a foreign country, seemingly useless in a strange school setting. And very vividly, my beloved children, I saw the hands of those who missed touching their loved ones when their dreams vanished. Your teacher."

A STRANGER AND A LOVED ONE

"One o'clock in the morning. Who would call me at this time?" I wondered. "Some bad news? One of my folks died? A student ran away from home? Or just a prank call?" I predicted the worst. I lay quietly counting exactly five rings. Then feeling increasingly uneasy I picked up the phone and said hello. A voice from the other end of the line answered,

"Is that you Ly? It's me. Mrs. Katz in apartment one."

"Are you O.K, Mrs. Katz?"

"No, I'm frightened, dear. This evening I saw a woman walking back and forth in front of our building. I can't sleep. I'm too scared. What do you think? Is she going to kidnap me?"

"What does she look like?"

"Large build, dressed in black from head to toes. I couldn't see her face."

"Don't you worry. She was probably looking for somebody's house."

"Really? I'm too frightened, dear."

"You will be all right." I assured her. Nothing bad will happen to you. Remember you have done a lot of good deeds. You are gentle and kind. Nobody would want to harm you."

That's right. I did help a lot of people. Are you sure I'll be okay? Is it true that nobody will harm me?"

"It's true, Mrs. Katz. Sleep tight now. Don't you worry about anything at all. If you need me, just give me a call. Anytime."

"Do you really mean it?"

"Yes. Anytime. I'll be there for you. Just remember you're not alone in this building."

"Are you sure? Yes. I'm sure. Have a good night."

I hanged up the phone, praying that she would sleep well. I said things to calm her down but I really know what she had done in her life to help others. I also hoped she would not call me late at night. I dared not to get out of my apartment during nighttime. Besides, helping an American like Mrs. Katz, who doesn't usually trust anybody, is risky. My skin color is different from hers. Would she trust me enough to let me help her? I remembered when I first moved into this building I spontaneously reached out to hold her hand in an attempt to support her walking up the stairway, she immediately withdrew her hand, looking at me uneasily. I sensed her doubt, stepping aside, waiting for her to slowly pass by me. I told myself I would be more careful offering help. She waved her hand as if she wanted to say good-bye, threw at me a suspicious look, and slammed her door.

I have had this look for many years without once that people refused my help. And yet she avoided me. I felt sad. For the first time in my life living in America, I realized I was a stranger. I don't look like people around me. Not only I had their physical features but also the same ways of interacting with others. I greeted people wholeheartedly. A brief question like "How are you?" would get me talking about how I really felt. The person I greeted had long gone before I realized it. Little by little I began to understand that people only say things out of politeness, and it is not necessary to hear the responses. Then I did the same. I said, "Hello", "Thank you" and walked away hastily. I am skillful to the point that I leave out the word "Good" in "Good morning" and only say "Morning" "Morning" to people and go on my way.

After months living in this building Mrs. Katz got to know me better. She allowed me to carry her grocery bags and agreed to let me throw out her trash. One day she said:

"You are my best neighbor. I love you. "

Since I have grown accustomed to being reserved I would not be excited at her compliment. I only smiled and thanked her. She pulled me down and made me sit next to her on the front door step to ask me about my work and my family status. The scene of the two of us sitting side by side on a bench in front of our building has become a regular happening. The story of her life had been repeated so many times that I know it by heart. She does not believe in men. She hates her first husband, despises the second one, and talks about her youngest son with bitterness. From her life experience, she gave me some contradictory and unconvincing advice,

"Listen to me, dear, listen to the experienced old woman. Don't you ever remarry. Just take good care of your son."

Then pointing at the ground, she laughed angrily as she was saying, "All the good men went down there. The ones who are alive on this earth want only one thing: having sex with the women they don't really care about. Luckily, I no longer have to worry about that part. I don't know about men in your country but here, in this country ...um... I do not guarantee. One certain morning or afternoon, out of the blue, they will tell you they want a divorce. You will feel so hurt that you pack up your belongings as quickly as you can."

Another time she said, "Listen to me dear, I love your little boy very much. He has compassion. He may turn out to be a good man. But you have to be careful. Don't be too good to him. His wife and children will be more important than anyone else, including you, his own mother. You should think of finding a husband for companionship in your old age. Most importantly, you have to marry someone who really love and respect you. You don't want to be like me. For years, I kept trying to please a stupid man. If I did not do what he wanted, he refused to take responsibility of a husband. Do you know what I mean?"

I did not really understand what she meant by "responsibility." I have come to learn that wives sometimes expect some kinds of responsibility from their husbands who might not be aware of. However, I nodded as if I were on her side. Encouraged by my agreement she enthusiastically continued, "In that case you should not get married. Take me as an example, since the day my husband entered the nursing home and died there, I have been free from troubles. I don't have to smell the stinky cigarette smoke or clean the messy toilet. I will never forget the time he woke me up early in the morning because he wanted me to be there for him at the nursing home. You know what time it was? "Six o'clock in the morning!"

I instantly thought of many Vietnamese women staying up late night after night to serve the in-laws patiently, but I did not say anything. I believed she needed to talk more than to listen to my comments. Instead, I told her to take care of herself and excused myself. She held my hand and said,

"You, too, honey, take care of yourself. Don't work too hard. I love you. You are an angel."

***

Winter came. Mrs. Katz did not come out to sit at the bench. Human voices, she only heard through different devices. Her television was on all day, her radio worked during the night, and the telephone would be used when she felt desperate. Having so much empathy for her situation I ventured to pay her a visit. She was delighted to see me, welcoming me as if I were her own daughter coming home from far away. Since that day every time she heard my footsteps she flung open her door to talk to me,

"You know dear, your son is precious. Yesterday I gave him a dollar for helping me carry my bag, he politely said he just wanted to be helpful. America would be a better country if only other children were like him."

I was surprised by such a big compliment, and I thanked her. Then she continued, "I see a lot of devils nowadays, no more real human beings. Children are spoiled rotten. In my time ...

Whenever she began with "In my time" I immediately found an excuse to get away because she would keep talking, and I was afraid I would be late for my appointments. Stopping me at her door to have a conversation has become a routine. So, when I was in a hurry I tiptoed by her door but it was thrown open and Mrs. Katz appeared. She said,

"You want to avoid me? You forgot me already? That's right. Who wants to remember an old woman?"

"That's not true. I ... How are you?" I replied.

"Still alive, still alive. I don't know when I 'll leave this earth. My friends have been gone one after another."

"Excuse me, Mrs. Katz, I have to go now or else I will be late for work."

Her dangling white hair, her dried and stoop body, and her cracked lips smeared with red lipstick created an image that haunted my mind. I thought of her in the midst of my teaching. I worried about here during the stormy nights. I pictured her body swaying, taking small steps on icy sidewalks between high heaps of snow. She has become a part of my life. I could not forget her and at the same time I did not want her to hope that we actually had a close relationship. I was afraid of a responsibility that I could not undertake. Being lonely she has transformed me, a stranger, into her loved one. And when she knew that I did

47

not meet her expectation she withdrew into her shell. She stopped opening her door to chat with me.

***

The winter has become wickedly cruel. The wind whipped violently, whirling the snow dust everywhere. All activities halted. Trees were bending bearing heavy bands of snow. It has been two months since Mrs. Katz was seen outside her door. As for me, I was too preoccupied with my own problems that I did not go to see her. The smell of accumulating dust mingling with different kinds of perfumes from her apartment was sometimes unbearable. There were days I had to hold my breath when passing by her place. And yet I was so afraid that one day that pungent smell would be replaced by a worse one, a smell of a forgotten corpse. I felt an urge to visit her. I knocked her door several times but there was no response. I raised my voice, "Mrs. Katz, it's me, Ly."

No answer. I knocked on the door harder and used an urgent voice to talk to her, "Mrs. Katz, are you home? I would like to see you."

The door was suddenly opened. Mrs. Katz stuck out her neck, came closer to me and with her trembling lips she uttered clearly and loudly into my ears, "You are a bitch!"

My stomach tightened. It was absolutely unexpected. However, her tone of voice did not sound mean. I guessed she was so mad at me that she reacted that way. I remembered one time she had called me an "angel." "It was all even out." I thought. With that in mind I tried to

48

comfort her, "Call me what you please as long as you are happy."

Realizing that I did not seem to be offended and also, she might be embarrassed for calling me a name, she raised her voice, emphasizing every single word, "YOU ARE A REAL BITCH. Why did you neglect me? I know I am an old hag, I can't attract anybody. Who cares about an old woman? And you wouldn't bother to be mad at me, right?"

Mrs. Katz turned around, walking unsteadily to the table. For fear of falling she pulled a chair and sat into it. Her purple and pink curlers were dangling from her thin hair, swinging gently back and forth to her agitated neck and her shortness of breath. The moment she looked up I had to hold my exclamation, "Oh God!" The bitter cold weather in New England compounded with an isolated life have changed her into a strange creature. The skin on her cheeks were sagging, pulling down the lower rims of her eyes, showing the redness beneath her watery eyeballs. The softness of her sharp nose drooped, nearly touching her dried and pale lips.

She waved her hand signaling me to sit down and asked me, "Are you hungry? Do you want a piece of toast or a cup of coffee?"

"I'm all set. Thank you."

"Are you sure?"

I looked at the plastic box, in which the noodles and the bean sprouts were soaking in thick and dark soy sauce, feeling queasy. I shook my head and asked her why she did not heat it up or cooked something for herself. She replied, "I haven't cooked for years. I only eat bread and a bit of cold cut. I can't even eat vegetables and fruits. Whatever I put in my mouth will rush out the other end a minute later. I am close to death now. Time flies fast. Let me tell you this. One morning I looked at myself in the mirror and I saw my hair all white, then I knew there was nothing else. You only need one certain morning, dear, to realize that."

I could not bear to hear what she said any more. I changed the subject, "I am here today because I need to talk to you about something that has bothered me."

She gave me a surprised look and said, "You need me? An old woman like me is of no help for anybody."

"You just feel that way, but you did help me a lot. You fought your boredom alone without bothering anybody."

There is no one for me to bother. I try my best each day. Even keeping myself clean exhausts me. How about you? What's the problem? I thought you came to see me out of pity."

"No. It's not that." I responded. "Actually, I feel sorry for myself. I don't know how to deal with hurtful feelings."

"What's the problem?" She asked, "Men, I am sure. I know you're a good woman the way you walk, the things you say, and how you laugh. Don't you give men your heart, they'll play with it and they will break it into pieces."

Mrs. Katz stopped talking. She was panting. I wanted to tell her that in my life there was a man who really made me happy. Therefore, I do not hate men yet. But I kept my thoughts to myself. I did not want to interfere with the

50

belief that she has nourished for a long time. I said something else, "Thank you for your advice. I will be careful with men. This time I have had some conflict with a woman. She is very pretty and also very angry. Every time she is upset about something she yells, screams, and humiliates the Vietnamese children. I recently confronted her because I could not stand it anymore. She is a friend of the administrators, who are now watching me."

"Oh my God!" Mrs. Katz exclaimed. "Are you okay? Would they fire you?"

"I don't know. They began to find fault in me. Even holding a pen during silent reading time was sternly reprimanded."

"Is she black or white?" Mrs. Katz asked.

"Caucasian. Here are some of the things she said to the Vietnamese children. "That boy needs more than human brains to be less stupid." "I pay taxes for you to be on welfare and you come to school to fool around. You come to this country flock by flock to look for food, don't you? "That girl over there is a real beauty! No hope to get into Harvard. Place her in special education classes." Do you know what special education is? It's a program for children with learning disabilities. A number of Vietnamese children were placed in the program because they did not know English!"

"That was so mean of her," Mrs. Katz said.

"I'm not sure she was mean. Just ignorant, I guess."

"Mean people say mean things, don't you understand? When did it happen?"

"I exploded lately. I used to explain to her what was going on in the lives of these children. She seemed to be receptive, but at times she could not control her temper."

"You are wrong. Let the tiger in you come out to deal with people like her. Don't allow them to step on you the first time."

"To tell you the truth I don't even know if I have a tiger in me."

"Yes, you do. Everybody does. You have to use it at the right time."

"You are probably right. I should have let her know my offense when the problem started."

Mrs. Katz breathed hard, pondering for a while and said, "Honestly, I really don't know what the right thing for you to do. If you confronted them you might lose your job. And that's not good, either." She released a deep sigh. I tried to comfort her, "I think I want to keep this job. I feel I have responsibilities to guide some of my students, who lost their parents during war time. I see myself as a mother trying to protect those children. They have just begun to learn English. Some of them kept smiling while they were being disciplined. When you don't understand another language, you appear stupid. They need me.

Mrs. Katz held out her hand to reach mine and said, "I'll pray for you."

"Thank you for your kindness. I am sorry to bother you with my stories. Please forgive me. I need someone to talk to."

I suddenly realized that I came to see Mrs. Katz because I feel safe to be with her, a white woman. I began to feel insecure around some Caucasians since the day at the meeting when I felt threatened by administrators. I grasped Mrs. Katz to help me kill the seed of discrimination starting to grow in me. I regretted I did so to her. The cold weather, my loneliness, and my heavy heart have made me drag Mrs. Katz out of her world into my struggling one. I stood up and gave her a kiss on her hollow cheek. With tears in her eyes, she embraced me and held me tightly as if she wanted to hold on to a life outside her world, a life that she was terrified of and yet she did not want to let go.

I closed my eyes, trying to sleep, but Mrs. Katz' image vividly appeared in my mind. I asked myself how I could live the rest of my life that I would neither be afraid of people nor need them so much. What should I do to shorten my last days and extinguish my long nights?

***

The rock music was blasting from my alarm radio. I got up quickly and jumped out of my bed. The first thing I did that morning was to water a withering plant.

A few months later Mrs. Katz was hospitalized. She had fallen and lay at the bottom of the stairway unconscious. She was very weak and could not recognize familiar faces. I thought she would never come home. But within a few weeks she was up and about and strongly refused to go to the nursing home. She once said to me she swore to God she would never go to a nursing home, where they just wanted money. The late Mr. Katz used to be charged for his hair cut twice a week and he actually had no hair to have cut!

Determined to die in her home she attempted to kill herself by turning on her gas stove. Her son had to hire someone to take care of her. Sometimes I head he painful scream "Help me! Help me!" but I did not do anything because I had met her nurse, who was wrongly accused several times for harming her.

One day, catching my sight through the gap of her door she called after me in a cold and sarcastic voice, "Hello, stranger, are you still around?"

THE MIRACLE "A"

Thanh was eleven years old. He came to this country a year ago. The child had only months of schooling in Vietnam. He had more experience of a street life than a caring family life. He had learned to get what he wanted by stealing, cheating, bargaining, and begging. Being smart he used all those tricks skillfully.

As a pupil in an American school he quickly learned about the merits of having good grades printed on report cards, honored names posted on bulletin boards, and admiration received from peers. He wanted to be the best and he believed he could become one. His problems were that he had very little learning skill and learning habit. He was also hyperactive and had difficulty paying attention.

I was his bilingual teacher. He applied his tactics to get an A from me. One time he stole my test draft. Other times he wrote words in his palms, on his sleeves or inside the hem of his shirt. His classmates reported he sat on a notebook. I was boiling with anger by being constantly cheated by him. I scolded him, gave him a couple of zeroes, ignored him, and even pleaded with him to do his homework. Nothing worked. One day I asked him, "Thanh, why don't you spend time studying instead of cheating?"

"It's so difficult to learn, Miss, and I want an "A" so badly."

His honest response gave me and idea, I said to him, "I tell you what I can do. There will be a spelling test in two days. Other children will have to know ten new words because they have been here longer than you were. You only need to know five words to get an "A." Would you like to do that?"

The child agreed.

I explained our situation to the whole class to justify what I had to do to help Thanh get what he really wanted. The majority of the class cheered. I then increased my assignments to him little by little. He beamed with each success, carefully placed his good work in a folder.

That was the story of my pupil's first "A"

Here is mine.

I hoped to get an "A" in the course I was taking. That would be the first "A" in my transcript in all those years I have studied in an American University. Different from my pupil I did not learn to cheat or to beg what I wanted. I simply worked harder than many of my classmates. However, for some reasons my highest grade stopped at an "A-." One of my classmates reminded me, "Minority is not priority." I did not buy to it. Professors, I believe, must be above that kind of discrimination. In some courses, I knew I deserved the best grade for my effort. But I also realized that due to the language barrier, my way of expressing myself, my cultural interpretation of ideas, and other missing requirements I might overlooked, my grades were not perfect. "I am a college student, not an illiterate child receiving favor from his teacher. Moreover, I am a teacher, I should not let the minus signs (-) beside the "A's" affect my life." I reasoned.

I probably did not care much about grades but this society or any societies did, and I found myself sometimes studying for grades more than for knowledge. I've tried to live up to social expectations with little self-satisfaction. Then one day to my surprise I saw a miracle "A" on my paper from one of the last courses of the program. I was even more surprised to know all my classmates got the same grade.

The professor explained, "From me you are all get A's because you have made it this far. Whatever grade you give yourself is your future."

AMONG STRANGERS

The woman wore different shades of green. Her multi-layer cape was flying in the gentle wind. A shed of bright light shone on her smiling face. She looked content and carefree. She had been ready for this moment a long time ago. Without any regret, remorse, or attachment, she gently lifted herself up and up, little by little, and disappeared into the vast sky. She was finally free from life stress and painful traumatic experiences. "What a wonderful image I had!" Mrs. K. said to herself, disappointed with her reality. She lay in the hospital bed trying to keep her body still for fear that the tubes attached on her would fall off. Triple bypass! Who would think a woman of her stature and simple life style, a candidate for an opened heart surgery! And yet she was.

The day before the operation she had a few visitors. Each one specialized in something important. A girl with long straight brunette hair and deep wrinkles on her forehead asked her permission to do a long-term study. She wanted to find out why Mrs. K. had blockages in her arteries because, according to the record, she was a non-smoker who did not have a history of overweight and other risk factors. Mrs. K. told the girl she would not normally refuse to help with this kind of study but she had to say "No" that time. She was dealing with her unfinished business and possibly death for the time being. However, she contributed what she has read: "How about stress, inflammation, or family medical history?" The girl nodded but appeared disappointed by missing a case study, said thank you to her, and left the room. The second one was a young rabbi. He wanted to know Mrs. K.'s religion and country of origin. He asked if she had anything to confide to him. It was his job to visit patients who needed major surgery. When he found out that Mrs. K. did not follow any particular religion and that she was quite pleased with what she had done in her life, the rabbi smiled and said it was very easy and pleasant to work with her. Then he opened a bible and asked her to put her hand on it while he was giving her his blessing. Next came the doctors. After giving their names, one said, "I am from the land of the Holy." The other chimed in: "And I am from the land of the Pope." Mrs. K. said: "I'm from Vietnam, the land of the oppressed. Save me!" We all laughed and off the doctors continued their round.

After the surgery, Mrs. K. had a severe side effect: Atrial Fibrillation. her heart beat so hard that she could see her garment going up and down on her chest. A series of test followed. During her unconscious state, she heard a soft and pleading voice saying over and over again "Wake up, sweetie, wake up for me, please!" Then she felt a small hand gently caressing her face. A surge of warm feeling went through her body and brought her back to consciousness. She opened her eyes and saw a slim girl with blonde hair and a cute nose smiling at her. "Who is this girl?" Mrs. K. wondered. "An angel on earth?"

Since they were both strangers from different continents Mrs. K. was surprised that the voice sounded sincere. She did not believe that the girl just did her job. There was something more. Her humanity? Her kindness? Whatever it was, Mrs. K. felt being loved and cared for.

Mrs. K. had another side effect. Her body could not take a certain kind of antibiotic. Her legs were swollen and her body was covered with rashes. The medicine made her sleepy. During her drowsiness, she saw a little girl who was unable to use her legs for walking. She rolled and crawled instead. To measure her strengths and weaknesses Mrs. K. had put a doll on one corner of her bed and asked her to get it. The girl started to crawl from the other side of the bed, but fell right away. She picked herself up, crawled a little farther, fell again, and rolled, and crawled, and rolled and crawled. With numerous trials and errors, she got to her destination. Her shining eyes widened with pride and joy.

Mrs. K. woke up feeling tears on her cheeks. The little girl, her client, was her savior. Mrs. K. was determined to overcome this traumatic experience.

***

It was past midnight. Mrs. K. was wide awake, listening to the buzz and the tic tic sounds of all kinds of machines mingling with the voices from some televisions in other patients' rooms. A shade of a slim figure passed by her rooms several times. She carried herself lightly with a serious and pleasant look on her face. The shade stopped at her bed, found her pulse, asked Mrs. K. how she felt, gently put her hand on Mrs. K's forehead, and carefully tugged her in.

"Dr. Olivia" Mrs. K. read the name tag the following morning, "Pretty young for a being a doctor, and beautiful, too." Dark smooth skin, big eyes, long nose, and full lips. This person bore the trait of an African. A colorful turban on her head made her look taller and elegant. "Who is she? A goddess?" Mrs. K. wondered where this doctor came from.

"No visitors? Did anybody call her?" One nurse asked another. "No. Oh, there was one. I asked for her name and she said 'Mom.' That's all. She sounded American."

"Really? Huh! This patient is an Asian, isn't she?"

Overhearing the nurses' conversation, Mrs. K. smiled, thinking of her Italian Mom whose daughter, Sarah, had brought home a Vietnamese friend from college forty years ago. Since then Mom has treated her like one of her own children. In her fifties, Mrs. K. felt protected by Mom as if she were a little girl. Mom Cristiani was the only one who called her regularly to find out how she was doing. Mrs. K. had put the name Rose Cristiani on her emergency information card. Whenever it came to the question of the contact person in case of emergency Mrs. K. had a hard time to make a decision. She was afraid to impose on her friends, who mostly had busy work schedules. Mom was a homemaker and she would go out of her way to do things for her. She even called to check on her on snow or hot days to see if she got home safely. Mom was always on her side too. Once Mom detected a sad voice from Mrs. K. she immediately asked: "Who hurts you? What a mean person she is!" "Mom, Mom, nobody hurts me. I'm just all

61

stressed out." Mrs. K. hastily responded. "Take care, honey. Come home for a hot meal, I have good soup and ricotta pie. OK, dolly."

Sometimes Mrs. K. cannot help asking herself how she ends up alone in this wide world but has not found the answers yet. "I'll think about this another time." She keeps postponing the response to this question. Of course, it is no fun to be alone most of the time, but she has gained her own freedom, which she enjoys tremendously. However, except for the comfort she found in the embraces of strangers, who were there for her when she needed them the most, the desire to have permanent love and care have not been fulfilled.

Returning to the work place after months in rehabilitation Mrs. K. received a warm and supportive welcome from her coworkers. "You look relaxed and happy. Take it easy, my friend. Remember not to carry heavy things OK! Let me hold that bag for you." Comments like those were repeated months and years after the incident.

Mrs. K. was alive and well. She decided not to dwell on resentments and the negative aspects of life. She would like to be more of a compassionate stranger.

HOME

Taking a quick look at my newly organized room I feel elated. Things are in places easy for me to see and to get when needed. On my left is the water view from a cove, and on my right, is a private bathroom. How convenient! I am sitting on my queen-size bed ready to watch a DVD on writing entitled "Put our heart on the page" by Anne Perry, a famous writer from Scotland. Writing is my thirst and I can't wait to learn from this experienced author.

The red-orange hue from the evening sunset and the quietness in my condominium add to my excitement of having a great time alone. The humming sound coming from the refrigerator is soothing. It's a new pricy one! I did it. After thirty years living in America as an immigrant starting from scratch I finally have a comfortable home for myself.

Wait a minute! Is this really my home? I ask myself. Right at that moment my mind brings me back to Vietnam where I used to live for almost half of my living years.

During the Vietnam wars our family moved to different places, but only the row house in a city once called Saigon where I resided for the longest time was the one that remains in my memory vividly.

It as a subdivision of about thirty houses called "Cư Xá Hòa Bình," meaning "Peace Residency" in English. Though it was away from the main street we could hear the repeated honking of the trucks, the puffing and starting of the motorbikes, the yelling of the drunkards, and the inviting callings of the peddlers: "Hot and crispy bread fresh from the oven here! ("Bánh mì nóng giòn mới ra lò đây!") "Who wants to eat sweet rice with beans?" (Ai ăn xôi đậu hong?") "Any loose pieces of precious metal, silver and gold crown to sell?" (Vàng vụn bạc vụn, răng vàng bể có bán hong?" Those voices still unexpectedly echo in my mind.

Entering our house, which was about fifty feet away from the opposite one, we stepped inside our living room where, there were an altar against the wall, a cupboard, and a large table with six chairs, mainly for guests. Behind the divided wall was others open bedroom where I shared a narrow space near the wall that separated the bedroom and the kitchen. From the window in the middle of the wall I could watch my mother's preparation for daily meals under a patch of sky through a transparent part of the roof.

I slept, studied, daydreamed, and suffered from my broken heart on a divan near the window. Smell from the cooked food with mingled flavors of ginger, garlic, lemongrass, and fish sauce lingered on my clothing, my hair, and my skin. Those flavors are now faded. I do not bother to find the special ingredients for each authentic dish.

Leaving the house for school or for work I was greeted by my neighbors, and occasionally they would spend a few minutes telling me about their concerns or praised me for my success, big or small.

Coming home I appreciated others welcoming gentle smile and the kind look in her eyes. She loved to watch me eat. She said the way I enjoyed food made her cooking less tiring. I am amazed by her courage for surviving through the catastrophe of the wars. They destroyed our houses and torn our family apart. My parents had eight children. Three of my older siblings joined the revolution to fight against the French war, then later went North with their fellow fighters who eventually became communists when the war had ended. They did not know much about me and I did not know about them, either. I only wished they would return home to look after me. But when they came back I was a career woman married to a publisher. My mother did not see my brothers and sister for more than twenty years. She supported the rest of us very much by herself. My father used alcohol to ease his emotional pain. Whenever facing a tough time, I visualized my mother's enduring smile. It helped me to get by.

I went back to Vietnam to attend my mother's funeral. Nothing in the house including the old furniture and the layout were changed since I had left my country for twenty years. The night after the memorial service I sat in front of an altar in the dim light of the candles looking at her photo intensely. I thanked her self-sacrifice for the well-being of the family and I told her with age and experience I understood her hope and dream. I told her I did try my best to realize her dream of being an educated woman who could write poetry. She was a natural. Without a formal education, she was able to instantly respond to my father's poems in oral verse.

I was with her spirit in that old, shabby house, which was no longer my home, and yet I wanted it to remain the same. I sat there for hours with mixed feelings of sadness and contentment of being alone with my mother the last time. I wanted that moment to last forever. A friend of mine once said I was a romantic fool. She warned me the harmful effect of acting on any kind of foolish romantic thoughts.

I heard my youngest sister already turned it into a three-story house with modern décor. I have never been there and I don't intend to revisit it. A romantic fool I was and I am.

So, do I really have a home? Why did I leave my country? Often times I heard the saying "The good earth will keep the birds." My land could be a good land for others, but it has not been for me. After North and South Vietnam reunited I worked as a translator in an art institute. My boss, a fanatical communist, was watching me closely. He believed anybody who received a scholarship from the United States was an American spy. He told the cleaning woman to take long breaks and made us, the clerical workers do her job. I thought of myself as a sparrow being mistaken as a vulture. I flapped my little wings and flew away.

Here, in a foreign country I don't have the love and care of my family. I don't have the warm welcome of my own fellow men as much as I need. The political history of my country has brought fears and much doubt among us. We treat one another with caution. A slip of the right or wrong word would be labeled as a communist or an anti-communist. To avoid trouble, I try to mind my own business and to volunteer doing social work.

Having no family members, I rely on my friends and mostly on me. I have planned the last years of my life in accordance to my physical, emotional, and spiritual needs. My current place is a place I want to hurry back after a trip. It has the comfort for an elder who does not want to be in anybody's way with her slow pace of doing things, her irregular wake time, and her up and down mood. It is a place where I can be free from the mundane in order to reserve energy for creativity. It is a place I call home.

"TAKE ME WITH YOU."

Relatives have repeatedly told me that I was very much like my mother. I take these comments as compliments. They said that I looked like my mother and behaved like her. As I get older and wiser, I have come to realize that the comparison is only somewhat correct. I feel proud of myself if I can resemble her in some small way. My mother passed away at the age of 102. None of her eight children was at her side when she died. She had lived with a paid caregiver for more than 10 years.

I flew home from the United States two days after she died. Alone in front of her altar, looking at her gentle face in a photo frame, I tried to put the pieces of her life together, and later, little by little, I could see her whole life's picture. A kind smile of people I've met will remind me of my mother. She greeted everyone with a smile, not just on her lips, but also in her eyes. She held their hands gently, expressing her affection, care, and warmth. Her charm attracted family members, neighbors, and acquaintances. In return, she received their attention, respect, and gratitude. My mother left us her good reputation as an amazing person. Whenever I made a friendly joke or a meaningful comment, people who knew her said I reminded them of my mother. Even an act of my kindness was said to be inherited from her.

Like my mother, I had a tough life. I endured a failed marriage, and for the most part of my life, loneliness. The men, my father and my husband, loved us but they were unable to help themselves. My father drowned himself in alcohol and my husband was stricken with anxiety disorder. We were left to be alone to construct and reconstruct our lives as well as to help those under our care. Her children and mine did care for us, but they all were busy pursuing greater dreams. Her older children joined the revolutions during the French war in the hope to gain the freedom and independence for our small war-torn country. And my son, who grows up in America is dreaming of establishing peace and justice for mankind.

One of the reasons we left our mother alone to take care of her own needs was that we truly believed she would overcome all obstacles without difficulty. In fact, however, she suffered. Whenever I experienced a broken heart, she was lovesick with me as if my lover were her own. That is small example. Her heart was repeatedly broken due to the many separations that kept her far from her eight children year after year. It seemed to me she had lived in our bodies through hardships, rejections, poverty, bitter marriages, danger, and dissolutions... The wars in Vietnam went on and on for nearly a century and her emotional pains followed her to the end of her life. "Take me with you!" she begged me again and again during my last visit.

I did not bring her to America. I was not in good health. I had a fulltime job, a heavy course load, a fatherless child, and an isolated life in a foreign country. I pictured my mother, who had been deaf for more than a decade, sitting alone at home during the New England winters, waiting for me and my son to come home. That was just another form of loneliness.

"Take me with you!" I heard that she would beg whoever came to visit her. My mother, a courageous and independent woman, who enjoyed outdoor and social activities, had lost her resistance to suffering, her zest for life, and her pride. She desperately needed help. My siblings and I did make sure that she was well fed and assisted with daily activities. But no less important, now that I am getting older, I realize she needed attention and an ongoing interaction with her family. She could not bear to be alone anymore. My mother died in a fetal position as an unborn baby. Her knees were too stiff to be stretched out.

"Take me with you!" was my mother's cry for help, but I could not really hear it when she was still alive.

A LETTER TO MY FATHER

Dear Father,

It's me Father, the tenth of your children. Remember Father, you used to call our names, one by one, telling us to line up every night before we went to bed. I couldn't wait my turn to stand in front of you to show you my worn-out outfit and to plead with you not to spend money on liquor anymore. Without a word, you slowly and repeatedly nodded your head and waved your hand to dismiss me. Now and then that image keeps showing up in my mind. In fact, I have a number of your photos stored in me. I saw you sitting night after night with bottles of wine next to you. Some were empty and some were half full. Your mouth was drooping, saliva dripping, cloudy eyes cast down, curly hair disheveled. You would sit there talking to yourself, cursing the war, blaming the country leaders for your misfortune, screaming in French at the enemy ghosts, who had destroyed your houses and torn your family apart. I heard you recite your philosophical poem, revealing your despair, and saying how much you loved my mother despite her not understanding you.

The photo that touched my heart the most was when I said goodbye to you to go to America. You were standing there in your hospital pajamas, waving your bony hand to me from far away. Turning around one last time to look at you, I saw the blurry shade of your frail figure in the evening's dim light, but your expression, Father, was clearer to me than ever. It said a lot about your love and care for me, your regret for not helping me during tough times, your sorrow for the separation that did not promise a future reunion. You had a terminal illness and I would be far away from you.

Dear Father, the other day when riding a bus to work I saw you sitting in front of a housing project in Cambridge. You looked like a statue with a lock of curly hair falling on your forehead. You seemed absorbed in your thoughts. There was no wine bottle next to you, just a walking cane. The bus passed a long way from you, but my mind was still there with you, or actually with an elder who much resembled you. Since that moment, I have been thinking of you, how kind and generous you were to others, how elegant and handsome you looked in your white suit, and how becoming you were in the setting of my grandfather's villa. As a child, I was lost in that enormous house with shining black lacquer furniture and grotesque animal heads hanging on the walls. I preferred spending time in our fruit-tree and flower gardens or riding in a canoe with my brothers under the moonlight, listening to the harmonicas they played.

The bombing destroyed it all. My siblings found how to survive and fight for the independence of the country. I was sent to the city to live with a relative. Remember, Father, when you found out that I was ill-treated there, you came to take me home. Father, you rescued me from being abused. I will always be grateful for that.

As I have more experience and a better education I believe I understand you, Father. The more my mother was praised for her virtue and heroic acts to hold the family together, the more you were blamed for your failure in business, your weaknesses, and your drinking. Now I understand, Father, year after year you were fighting the demon of alcohol addiction, which ruled you and destroyed your will to be a great man, a man who took good care of his family, who against all odds and adverse situations, re-established his inherited kingdom and helped build the war-torn country. But the demon won the battle and you became a lost soul.

Dear Father, your soul will never be lost in mine.

Love,

Your daughter.

ASHES

Today is Sunday and the third day of the Lunar New Year. Brother Six passed away four days ago, I dragged my feet back and forth in my apartment. Going to the kitchen I opened the refrigerator. Nothing appealed to me, only a stale portion of bread and some wilted vegetables. I was hungry, remembering I skipped supper yesterday. Carrying myself to the living room I deliberately dusted the book shelves. Entering the bedroom, I reluctantly made my bed. Winter is bitterly cold in Boston this year. The chill is running through me. Where will I go today? No yoga sessions. No Vietnamese language classes to teach. I was left alone with the memories of my deceased brother. His image was appearing more vividly than ever. I saw a bony elder with dull eyes and hollow cheeks, wearing an oversized shirt spotted with dried blood from blistered skin. I saw him lying in a smelly dirty bed in a senior home for unfortunate people. To break the unbearable silent atmosphere, I placed a CD into the CD player. A piano playing the song "How deep is the ocean" sounded like heavy drops of rain inside my heart. How deep is my sadness? It is now floating, flowing with the waves of my unrest feelings. I should not be alone in this state of mind. I called Pam to break the news. Americans do not mind receiving the bad news on the first days of the Lunar New year like many Vietnamese do. Pam came to pick me up. We have been colleagues and good friends for years. We have shared our private lives freely without being concerned about jealousy or bad mouthing.

Facing each other in a quiet restaurant Pam began to ask me about my brother. I described his physical condition and told her I realized that nothing lasts forever, including our bodies. But my brother's death shook me deeply because it was as pitiful as his life. There were no loved ones with him, no funeral, and no memorial service. My niece wrote to me:

"My dear aunt, my uncle was gone! It is heartbreaking not to be able to see him a last time. When my family arrived, we were informed that his body had been cremated. They said they had to do it quickly to get ready for the New Year celebration! The file read: No family, no home, and no identity information. The employees here told us he had been brought to this place when found wandering in front of a hospital."

I lost contact with him a few months ago, when he was first hospitalized. I tried different ways to reach him but without much success. On the phone, I only heard unintelligible words and scream of his frustration. My letters and greeting cards were not replied to. No news to say he received my money, either.

Pam sighed and said, "I'm sorry for his misfortune. I guess that's what happens in any country to old and poor people with no family. Who did he live with and what did he do for a living?"

"I was told that the French war was going o during his time and because of his learning disability he was kept at home to do chores. He could be trusted to walk children to schools and to accompany older relatives to hospitals. He used to live with my brother Four, a painter, who had passion for his art work and led a wild life. They lived together for more than thirty years, enduring each other's temperament. One as decisive and fast, the other slow and stubborn."

"How about other family members?" Pam asked.

"We all tried to help, but I guess the main thing is an individual has to help himself. My brother lacked that survival capacity. He was unable to keep the house I gave him when I had left for the United States. I really do not know who took it from him."

I paused to think, had a sip of water, and continued, "You know Pam, because all his life he was never able to hold a job long enough, he received no financial support from the government.

Pam shook her head and said, "It's really sad! What was his diagnosis?"

Her question made me wonder. I kept silent for a while then answered, "As far as I know his mental issues were unattended. 'Tender heart and cloudy mind' was how I thought of him. He couldn't make decisions for himself or stayed focused to complete a small task. He would stop several times during work and smile about something that might amuse him. Whenever my mother reprimanded him for not doing a good job, he got really angry and became argumentative, saying nobody understood him. He blamed my mother for all his difficulties. I heard him repeatedly said these lines to my mother: "I don't want you to give birth to me. I don't want to have me in this life." My mother just looked at him painfully every time he reproached her and left the room. He followed her, bickering. She knew him well enough not to reason with him. When being confronted, he would bang his head against the wall."

I heaved a deep breath, trying not to relive the bloody scenes. Pam looked at me with empathy. Her willingness to listen to my story encouraged me to say more, I began telling her some memorable anecdotes that happened long ago. My brother died at the age of eighty-one. I am eight years his junior.

"I never will forget the time he sat next to my bed when I was sick and pleaded with me to get well. And even though he was afraid to leave the house he did try to go out to look for me when sometimes I did not come home. My friends were very touched by his concern for me. Those who knew my brother remembered him as a nice and caring person. Once he was badly battered due to some misunderstanding, he called out loud to warn the person who hit him to run away when he caught the sight of a policeman!"

We both dabbed our tears.

"Well, it sounds like he was such a good person." Pam said. "My deepest sympathy for you, Mai. It hurts terribly when you lose your loved ones, but his death actually liberated him and his family as well. Please take care of yourself. Feel free to call me if you I can be of any help."

I stood up, smiled gently and said, "It's rush hour. We better leave. Thanks for the free therapy session. I really need someone like you to talk to. I very much appreciate your kindness."

"My pleasure. Anytime."

***

The minute I entered my somber quiet apartment I turned on the lights and the heater, changed the CD and listened to the song Nostalgia, playing by a musician named Yanni. The melody started slowly as if walking you back to time. Suddenly, it rushed unceasingly as if catching what was going to disappear. Then without any lingering notes, it abruptly ended. I turned off the music and sat at my desk, quickly writing this story, hoping to leave some trace of my brother behind.

As I was about to stop writing, suddenly in my head I heard the tune of a Vietnamese song entitled "Cát bụi" or "Dust" composed by Trinh Cong Son." The lyric says, "What particle of dust changed into you, and again you'll become another dust particle. ..." Reincarnation? I haven't given much thought about it until now.

My beloved brother,

Before we say farewell, I would like to let you know something that I have told anybody. I have longed to practically make your life joyful and to understand those who share your fate. If only your kind heart could have made up for whatever was missing in your brain! But no, the Creator had his own plan. It is said everything happens for a reason. You are one of the reasons for me to pursue further education in order to become involved in the lives of special-needs children. As long as my mind is intact I'll not stop trying to be helpful to them. Then my dear brother, in the end though you and I will be reduced to ashes, we really are useful beings, aren't we?

Your sister,

Mười

A COLD

"Hello, I'm an interpreter. The snowstorm is really bad. I can't come to the hospital. The doctor asked me to ask you a few questions. Please tell me your name, your age, and how you are feeling."

"My name is Nhân Hoàng, 28 years old. I'm not sick, just trembling."

"Are you cold?"

"No, I'm not cold because it is cold. I have four or five layers on me, shirts and pants and all. I'm just trembling."

"Do you have a cold... no, no, ... I mean do you have a temperature, a headache, do you cough or sneeze?"

"No. I'm fine. My heart, my lungs, and my liver... they're all in good condition. I just feel cold, very cold inside."

"Please let me talk to the doctor."

. . . .

"Dr. Gordon, the patient said he was trembling and that he felt cold inside."

"Ask him if he is on medication and how his living condition are."

. . . .

"Hello, Mr. Hoàng, the doctor wants to know if you have taken any pills."

"No, I have no pills to take. Please tell the doctor to give me some medicine that can help me to be healthy, to look rosy and happy like everyone else."

"How's your sleep Mr. Hoàng?"

"I have no good food to eat, and no good place to sleep, therefore I don't eat well and I don't sleep well. Please tell the doctor not to waste his time diagnosing me. I know I am not well because I don't have enough food to eat."

"Are you hungry now? Is that why you are trembling?"

"I can eat, but really I don't have to eat right now. Only if food was there at mealtime. Three meals a day like everyone else. Even two meals are okay for me, Miss."

"Who are you living with?"

"I have nobody to live with."

"Where do you live?"

"Nowhere. I live where I am. Please tell the doctor to give me some medicine. Other doctors in other states gave me some. I don't know what kind, but they help me to sleep well, to look rosy and happy like everyone else. Please tell the doctor I feel cold inside. Every night I tremble. It starts from the inside, and my body shakes."

"Pease let me talk to the doctor."

. . . .

"Dr. Gordon, it sounds like he took sleeping pills or antidepressant in the past"

"Is he psychotic? What do you think? How's his speech?"

"It's hard to tell. He's polite and his speech is coherent. The unusual thing is he kept repeating he wanted to be rosy and happy like everyone else, and feeling cold inside."

"Ask him if he drinks."

. . . .

"Hello, Mr. Hoang, the doctor wanted to know if you drink."

"Miss, I don't drink, I'm not on drugs, no stealing, no killing. I only feel cold inside. I know my problems because I used to work in a hospital in Vietnam. I'm a decent man. Please tell the doctor to kindly help me find a place to live, a job, some relatives, a few good friends, and best of all, a country. Please do tell him so. I'll be very thankful to you."

....

"Doctor, the patient said he didn't drink or do drugs. He said...

"Ask him if he is allergic to any drugs."

"Doctor, he said...

"Ask him why he came to the hospital."

"He said he needed some medicine. He felt cold inside and he needed help to have enough food and...

"Tell him to talk about his illness."

....

"Hello, Mr. Hoàng, the doctor asked you....

"Please, Miss, please tell him to give me some medicine to help me look rosy and happy like everyone else. Tell him I'm fine, I only feel cold inside. My voice is shaky sometimes. My body is trembling. I feel trembling inside.

....

"Kim, what did the patient say?"

"He still repeated the same lines I had mentioned to you."

"Alright then. Thank you. We just wanted to know if he is under influences. I'll refer him to the Psychiatry Unit."

"Doctor, he said…

"Thank you very much. Merry Christmas!' Click. …hum…hum…hum…

EDNA

"Downtown Boston. This is an express bus," the driver told me.

"I know. Thank you."

"Come on, lady. Get on the bus. The weather's bad, isn't it?"

"Yes, it's really bad." I concurred.

"Oh… oh… oh… Sorry. I'm tired today. I keep yawning and yawning." She covered her mouth and continued,

"Never mind. I'll yawn with you. I'm tired, too."

"I can't wait to go on a vacation. This time I'll go to Hawaii. Have you ever been to Hawaii? It's paradise. I'll lie on the beach all day with my boyfriend. I'll do nothing. Completely nothing. Just eat, sleep, and enjoy the sun. Oh! Hawaii! The blue sky and the green trees! It's wonderful! Especially when you're with your boyfriend."

"I'm happy for you," I said.

"I'm happy for myself, too. Five years with that bastard husband of mine, the lazy, dirty, treacherous drunk. I had enough. I finally got rid of him."

"Do you have children?" I asked.

"Children! Thank God, I don't have any. Everything is so expensive nowadays and I wouldn't dream of having children with a jerk like him. The divorce was over last year. What a relief! You know, if you keep searching you'll find one. I found one for myself already. He's wonderful! I love him. Oh yes, I sure love him. He's … he's… white, you know."

The woman lingered for a few seconds, cocked her head to look at me as if she wanted to know my reaction to what she had said, and continued

"… A wonderful white man. Look, look over there, you see that corner? That's where we have our break. Just the two of us. Sometimes he buys me a cup of coffee and a doughnut. He's just so nice! Oh, I love him."

"Does he also drive a bus?" I asked.

"Yes," She said. "His bus is right behind us now. There! There! Did you see him? He's so nice! You know what he did the other day? He gave me a rose when he passed my bus. He always makes me happy. He cooks for me when I'm tired. We do things for each other, you know. That's the way it should be. I just love him."

I no longer thought of my tiredness. I began to really notice the woman. Her southern accent was so different from the Bostonians' that I found difficult to understand thoroughly what she was saying. Her voice was low and sonorous. This must be a good voice for singing, I thought. She had a little overbite. Her teeth were extremely white and even. The rouge applied on her cheeks became the color purple mingled with a sort of red shade, dotted with some dry pimples on her black skin. Her very short curly hair was nicely cut. Her small eyes, lined with curled and thick eyelashes were actively moving in   the rearview mirror. I noticed the black and white design on her square plastic earrings. She had on her firm body a very neat uniform that went well with her man-like, shining shoes. Her hips were rather big and her legs seemed longer than they were supposed to be. She handled the bulky bus as easily as a child driving a miniature car. She honked the horn, swore here and there, and moved her head back and forth to talk to me, the only passenger on her bus that day.

The bus was coming out on a highway. The wind swept through the openings of the windows.

"Where are you going?" She asked me loudly.

"I'm going to school," I screamed back to answer her.

"Still go to school? You are too ambitious! What do you do for a living?"

"Teaching."

"Really? You don't look like a teacher. Not tough enough. How are you able to handle kids?"

I smiled slightly and answered, "It's the end of the day. I'm too tired to look tough."

"Are you married?"

"Yes, once. I have a son. His father died."

"Oh, I'm sorry. I didn't uh…uh."

"That's alright. It has been a long time since that happened. I don't really remember anything, anymore."

"Good. Shouldn't remember things that make you sad. You have a boyfriend?"

"No."

"How come?" She asked me with doubt in her voice, and glanced at me observantly. "You're just kidding me, aren't you? A nice lady like you? No boyfriend?"

"Actually, I have had a few at different times but it just didn't work."

"Why not? You must be too choosy. Let men love you and care for you. If one is not good to you, find another."

In an effort to show her my gratitude for her concern I tried to explain my "fault" of not having a boyfriend.

"As you know," I said, "things don't seem to work the way we want. The men we meet are either too old or too young. The ones we love don't love us. The ones we don't do. Then there are those we like but don't love, or vice versa. Something like that."

"Yes. That's life. Don't I know life too well! That's why I enjoy whatever I have, and forget what made me unhappy. In a few more years when I'm forty-five, I'll retire from this job. Excuse me! I've worked long enough. Life is too short, you know."

As she stopped to talk to the toll collector on the highway, I bent my head, letting myself sinking into deep thought: A woman, experienced in driving buses, had luxurious vacation at different nice places, dumped the past, carrying life with radiant smiles and an open heart...

Suddenly the bus gave a jerky move, and I heard her asking loudly, "Are you sleeping? Did you see anything? I just flirted with the man in the booth!"

"Did it work?" I asked casually.

"Of course," she answered, looking somewhat proud of herself. "Just for the fun of it, you know. He's a nice guy. Men are too lazy to flirt nowadays. We women have to be a little forward."

I was going to tell her that most women in Vietnam are sleeping beauties, waiting for princes to come kiss them on their eyes. Therefore, there are many women with gray hair on their head still waiting for their princes to come. Whoever has the courage to wake up and go look for one is thought of as a woman of low class. But it was too lengthy to say so. I made it short instead.

"I'm afraid if we are forward they will think less of us."

I could sense anger in her voice when she answered me, "Why less? Are they really better than us? Nobody is special. Everybody is the same. All people are equal."

I looked out of the windows to a far distance, feeling dejected. Even if I spent the rest of my life thinking about the word "equality," I knew I would never believe in it.

Noticing my mood, she thought I was upset. She slowed down the bus and tried to comfort me.

"Really," she said, "you have got to have a boyfriend. Let me find one for you. It must be hard to live without one. How do you feel about it? Do you have any relatives in this country?"

"No."

"Then why did you come here?" Her voice was edgy. "When are you going back to your country?"

"I can't go back." I said sadly.

"Why not?"

"Because I am Vietnamese." I answered her with a shaky voice, trying to hold back my tears.

"Why can't Vietnamese go back to their country?"

"After the wars, came the communists. I am not their people. They used me but they never trusted me. They were suspicious of those who had something to do with the Americans. Many years ago, I had come to this country ago as a student, and then I went back to Vietnam. I always want to be a good citizen, living in my country, serving my people. I wanted to stay there but I had to leave for America. You know something, in my country… "

I intended to pour out my feelings about my country, but she already interrupted me. One hand on the steering wheel, the other waving furiously in the air, she spoke angrily,

"The wars. I don't understand why there are wars. Why do people have to fight each other? I'm just so mad. Men have become heartless. And why is there discrimination? I'm telling you. This world is crazy. I don't understand why there are wars…"

I did not hear what she was saying anymore. I was thinking: This woman is still angry because of the wars. I was surprised at her anger. It was as if war only happened just yesterday for the first time on this earth! For me war has been going on for a long time, from my father's generation and from my grandfather's. It is no longer an anger I feel, but an everlasting endurance of pain and bitterness. And now because of war it is the endurance of an exile life that I'm leading. It is eroding my soul; causing me physical pain and making me feel estranged from my people back home. Next is the endurance of the injustice and discrimination that I have to deal with in this country.

"Get rid of the Vietnamese!" So often I have heard that line. It hurts deeply to feel rejected. The longtime lasting endurance has shaken my spirit, taken away my vitality and my optimism in life... No! I shouldn't go on thinking about those things. I need to save some energy to sit through the two-hour lecture of this evening's class. There will be tomorrow and the day after tomorrow. I should avoid those thoughts. I have to finish school. That is important. I have to know English well enough to protect myself from being pushed down by unkind people. I have to make a living for my son and myself. I have to help my needy friends and my folks back home. I really don't have the energy to think of war, of peace, of love, and it seems my soft heart is becoming tougher and tougher with time. I held the armrest of the chair to push myself up from the seat, said goodbye to the woman, and got off the bus. She had probably stopped talking a while ago. She looked at me kindly and said goodbye to me warmly.

Each time I was on her bus she talked to me about life and about people, as enthusiastically as ever. Most of the time I was quiet, giving much thought to what she said, analyzing it, comparing and contrasting it to my thinking and my beliefs, and occasionally giving out a deep sigh.

There was one time when, seeing me waiting for the bus, she drove past me swiftly and stopped, waiting for me. I ran to the bus, panting. We both laughed. She said to me,

"Did you have a good run, lady? What do you teachers do that you always look so tired? Have you been out drinking and fooling around at night a lot?"

We giggled gleefully. The passengers on the bus showed different reactions as they were watching us. A young girl smiled. Some middle-aged ladies frowned slightly. The men and the boys seemed unaffected. An old Italian man repeatedly nodded his head. I got used to and began to like all the expressions of endearment she used to address me. She called me 'sweetheart,' 'honey,' and even 'baby'. ("Hello sweetheart! Be careful, honey. Is something bothering you today, baby?")

Another time she did something that deeply touched my heart. That was the day I did not have to go to my evening class. I was on my way home from the supermarket, carrying heavy bags of groceries. Suddenly, I heard lots of loud honking on the street. I raised my head, searching for the cause of all the noise. Her bus was parked right in the middle of the street, and many other cars were waiting for her to move. In spite of the honking coming from all directions and the questioning looks of the passengers, her bus remained in the same position. Waiting until my eyes caught hers, she threw her head in a manner to tell me to get on the bus quickly. The honking made me nervous. I shook my head and waved my hands pointing at the building ahead of me to tell her I did not need a ride. She gave a long goodbye honking. I looked after the bus until it was out of sight. My heart was filled with happiness.

Then there was a time I did not go to class because I had a bad cold. When we saw each other again she appeared to be cross and sarcastically told me that I was sick only because I fooled around too much. I explained to her honestly that my shortcoming was that I really didn't know what 'fooling around' was like. My life was a cycle of studying and working, and working and studying. She gave me some advice about health care and kept telling me over and over again to take better care of myself.

The last time I was on her bus I said to her,

"Today is the last day of my course and you'll be assigned to a new route soon. We may not see each other during my next semester. I think we should say goodbye now." I stepped closer to where she sat. She threw out her arms and raised her face, waiting for a kiss. We gave each other a big hug and parted with warm and caring kind words. Then I said to her,

"My name is Kim. What's yours?"

"Edna. It's a strange name but for sure... it's my name."

When the good-bye honking was no longer heard and the sight of the bus disappeared into a faraway distance, I cast my eyes down, letting them follow my slow steps and mumbled, "Edna."

"Edna, you are a friend. You have made me feel welcomed in a country that I thought would always be a land of strangers!"

PRAYERS

In a book

I remember I read these lines in an American veteran's memoir:

"Dear God, help me. I killed them, many of them. After all those years, I still see children's eyes wide open in shock and instantly close forever. You know God, like them I'm also a victim of the war in Vietnam. I was sent to that small country to liberate the people from communists. I bombed their villages. Now I'm ready to go back there to apologize for the damages and the suffering I caused to them. I am scared, God. I' afraid for my own safety. Please help me to do the right thig, God."

At a friend's house in Vietnam

I heard the following saying when visiting a friend. She stood in front of an altar talking to her deceased husband,

Old man, it's your tur to care for your children. I raised them by myself. You know how hard it has been for me to feed five mouths in the family. You know how small and weak I am. You know why I had to bribe your enemy to save your life. You know who cared for your sick parents during the many years you were held as a political prisoner. You know how I got the money to help you escape from the country by boat. You lost the war and I lost my dignity. And yet you had to die at sea! I pray to your soul to make your sons' trips to freedom safely. All my life I did not ask you any big favors. But now it's your turn. They've joined other boat people and they're on their way. You have to look over them, you have to watch every step of your children the rest of their lives. You hear me, old man? So saying she brought her palms to the center of her heart and bowed several times to her husband's photo.

In a street of a small town in America

An elder held a rosary in her hand while walking and mumbling. Tears trickled over her hollow cheeks. I passed by her, then walked back to see if she needed help. We spoke the same native language, Vietnamese. She shared with me what has bothered her,

"I pray to Christ not to let them kill my grandchild. I found out they had sent the girl to England. With their money, they can marry off their daughter easily. My son has gone mad losing his girlfriend with child. I know he is no doctor or engineer, but he is such a sweet and kind young man. The war took his leg and left a wound in his heart. I was so happy someone accepted my son who he is. The girl loves him. But now . . ." The lady let out a deep sigh, wiped her eyes, and asked me if by any chance, I was on my way to the church down the street. I wasn't but I said yes.

Once we were inside the church she lighted the candles and hastily moved from one statue to another. She caressed the feet of the saint figures. She tugged the money under the cradle of baby Jesus. She kneeled down, looked up at the Christ statue hanged on a cross, and totally lost herself in prayers.

In an elementary school in America

An eleven- year-old boy sat silently in a counseling room for quite a while. His body stiffened and his eyebrows knitted together. I was patiently waiting for him to vent. All of a sudden he raised his fist, slammed the table and said, "When I grow up I'll be a soldier. I'll kill that man. He is my fake father. My real one was killed on a battlefield. My mother promised not to have anything to do with men but she did not keep her promise. I heard him telling my mother, "Quiet! The boy can hear you!'" He paused, breathed hard, and continued, "I know Buddha's teaching tells us not to kill any living things. But I already asked Buddha to forgive me. I killed the insects because they bit me. I'll kill that man because he hurts my mother. I hear her moan and scream. He stole her money and makes her work hard. Buddha knows everything. He knows I'm a good boy."

SUFFERING

"Do you know what ocean means?" Hoang, my new friend asked me over the phone. *What is this woman trying to say? Maybe she wants to start a conversation with an analogy as he has done before.*

I'm listening." I said.

"Have you ever on a cruise ship right in the middle of nowhere and you saw no land, no trees, nothing but water around you? That is an ocean. It's infinite. I'm telling you, life is an ocean of suffering."

"Yeah, I've heard that line many times."

"But you would not understand it unless you were in my situation," she sighed.

"What situation?" I was tempted to ask her but I held my tongue and waited.

"Ken, my youngest son, the one who chatted with you at the last party, died suddenly. I'm calling to ask you to be with us at the funeral. I was glad he had finally come around to make a connection. He seldom shared his thoughts. You knew him. You know how nice and kind he was. Oh! My smart, sweet son!" she sobbed.

I went to the Buddhist Temple for her son's memorial service. Small talk and whispering with hinted responses here and there gave me bits and pieces of the cause of the young man's death. Some said he overdosed. Others thought he committed suicide. A few people shook their heads and uttered the words "Unknown reason."

When being pressed for an answer the mother confided, "Whatever the cause of this death was, I, his mother, knew all along he had suffered for more than twenty years, and we, his loved ones, were all affected by his misery. She heaved a deep sign and continued, "In a way I am relieved that he is free from pain. He has paid off his life debt."

"Who are you?" A man looking quite lost asked me.

"I'm a friend of the mother. And you?"

"I'm the father." He said with an air of confirmation.

"Oh!" I exclaimed, trying to suppress my surprise.

I had heard a lot about this man. I guessed he seemed to be lost because he was out of the family picture for years. His present young wife repeatedly rejects him and his ex-wife has moved on with her life. He has tried to reconnect with his estranged family without success.

"You live around here?" He asked.

"Yes. Sorry, I have to go. Good bye." I said as I was running to a friend who called me to hurry for a ride.

Turning around I saw him walk away from the crowd, alone.

Later I told Hoang I had met her ex-husband.

"What's your impression about him?" "I feel sorry for him but he deserves the punishment. You know he had discreetly cleaned all our assets, left me with five children and a run-down house, and gone back to Vietnam to marry a girl about his oldest daughter's age. When we first came to America I took many menial jobs, working seven days a week and going to night school to learn a career. With my support, he got a college degree, made good money, but was terribly stingy and very controlling."

"It's amazing how you've survived!" I said.

"For the love of my children I've got to be sane. Of course, it cost my health. I have all sorts of ailments now because I tried to endure the hardship for years. Also, the drugs I took including the anti-depressant ones for treatment of my craziness messed up my system. The bastard did not know I was beside myself for a long, long time. "So, what do you think about him?"

"When I asked him how he related to your family he looked sad and distant. I don't know if it was my imagination or the tone of his voice, which sounded like he firmly claimed his right as a father who suffered a tragic loss of a son."

"Too bad and too late! Ken took the divorce much harder than my other children. I guess he grieved for his loss and for mine, too. He loved me dearly. He quitted school, hung out with the wrong crowd and became addicted to drugs. His older siblings and I tried our best to save him but … Oh well, it was his fate. At best he is free from suffering of guilt and craving of drugs."

All of a sudden I felt weary. I sensed the agony of the deceased. I could not take any more unbearable details. I asked to excuse myself.

What is it about me that I feel the pain of others as if it were my own. When I saw someone have a cut I felt like I was bleeding. One time I thought I fell when detecting a man hanging on outside a tall building. Then I realized that he was doing his job.

Hoang story reminded me of the anxious look of a second grader, who told me she was afraid her mother would go blind because she had cried days and nights. Her father spent much of his time behind a locked door to chat with his young girlfriend in Vietnam. She asked me to teach her mother the coping skills she had learned from me, her school counselor. "My mother does not know what to do but cry. She speaks little English, works at a nail salon from nine to nine, and does not drive. She's afraid of my father. He takes all her money. Please help my mother."

Her pleading voice at times resounded in my mind. Her anxiety worried me. Her mother's aguish gave me pain. Suffering is like some kind of disease that spreads.

Nights fall. Days break. Time is going by. Sooner or later everybody will die. And yet people keep hurting people one way or another, not to mention many have the need to end others' lives or their own sooner. I've seen and heard too many tragedies. I feel drained. Does suffering have no end or will human desire and hatred continue to cause suffering?

BUYING HAPPINESS

"Hello auntie, I'm going to Wrentham Village to return a dress. It didn't look good on me. It's heavy, too. I really like the color. I want to give it to my sister but I'm not sure if she likes it. You come with me, ok. No, you can't. That's ok, too, I'm so used to go "se-low" anyway."

"Slow?" I wondered what she meant by using the word "slow" in this context. Then I couldn't help flick a smile realizing that she wanted to say "solo." She spoke Chinese and Vietnamese fluently but little English. Over the phone, I promised to go with her another time but she immediately talked over me with an urgent and pleading voice, "Come. Go for a ride. It won't take long. Come. Come. OK. Get dressed now."

Against my will I agreed. I remembered I owed her a favor. She gave me a ride to the airport on a snowy day. Besides, she is the only Vietnamese speaking person in my neighborhood and she considered me a relative, calling me "auntie." Fifteen minute later she picked me up and off we went. She drove fast and used her brake abruptly. She made the car stop and start so sudden frequently that my head was thrown back and forth. Thanks to the seatbelt my body was held in place. Her speech and her driving speed went well together. I found myself saying "Uh" ... Uh" "Yeah... Yeah" over and over again. There was no hope for me to interrupt her talk or to voice my opinion.

"Do you think I am a good person? My friend needed 10,000 dollars. I went to the bank, withdrew the money and gave it to her. She was robbed, losing all her cash saving. I felt sorry for her. We have been good friends."

I was going to say: "It's too bad." Or "It's very kind of you." But she was already on another topic: "I'm tired of working in the nail salon. The owner is very young, in her twenties and already very rich. She worships a four-face Buddha statue and she gets all the luck she needs. Stingy. Just plain stingy. Wouldn't let me use a clean, fresh towel for a new customer. Wouldn't turn on the air conditioner on a hot day. And yet lots of people come to her salon. Four-face Buddha, you know. It works for her. Damn her. I want to get married. One of the customers I do message weekly is interested in me. He much older, but I don't mind. I only need him to pay the rent and the health insurance. I'll take care of the house and cook him good food."

"Are you sure that's what you really want?" I asked.

She did not answer my question, making a quick turn and cursing the driver in another car. She turned her head towards me, said "sorry", and asked me if I was all right.

Appreciating her concern, I took a close look at her and began to notice her appearance. Reddish short hair shaved above her nap and jelled the top gave her a youthful look. She had fair skin, seemingly unnatural full cheeks and full red lips, a nose job, and dark tattoo eyebrows and eyelids. She reminded me of a Chinese movie star photo on the cover of an entertainment magazine. Her teeth were unusually white and even. In her trendy flowery see-thru sleeveless blouse with deep cleavage, showing her full breasts, she looked appealing for her age. I complimented her look. She seemed to enjoy what I said but immediately denied it.

"Youthful no more. I'm nearly 53."

Then she sighed. It did not take her more than two minutes to start another conversation, revealing her true self,

"You know, I'm a faithful and caring person but I have a hot temper and when my blood is boiling with jealousy I go crazy. I once chased my boyfriend with a knife in my hand when I found out that he had been married before. He was so afraid of me that he disappeared for good. I haven't seen him again since then. I love him. I can't sleep with anybody I don't love. That's why I'm still single."

By then we arrived the parking lot of the shopping mall. She heaved a deep breath and resumed her talk about her choice of buying things. The minute we stepped inside a clothing store she rushed to one aisle after another, darting her gaze to all the racks loaded with colorful clothes around her. She felt the materials, tried on different styles, and commented on each item: "This does not look elegant on me." "That one is ok but too expensive. I have to wait for a sale.", "Oh, I hate this bulging stomach. Got to have another surgery to rid the fat." She pulled her blouse up and pinched her belly skin. I told her I would meet her at the car in an hour. She said "two hours." I nodded. A negotiation with her would be in vain, I thought.

When we finally left the mall, she asked me how much I spent. She said she did not spend more than 500 dollars, and she deserved it, because she worked hard for it. She explained that she did not really buy things for herself only. She bought them for her sister and her nephews, who reside in Hong Kong and Vietnam, where she lived for the most part of her life.

On the way home, she asked me if I was tired. She asked me if I wanted to share a room in her condo because she would trust an educated roommate like me. She would take care of me when I was sick, telling me to call her whenever I need a ride or a homemade meal. In return she wanted me to keep her company and to help her with her English. She was afraid that her limited understanding of the language might cause mistakes when dealing with the banks, the stock, and the credit card companies. She did not want to lose a penny she had been earning for years with her hard work and perseverance. She was tired of breathing the strong smell of the nail polish day after day. She was fed up with her other job as a masseuse. She hated to message "the thing" of some male customers if requested. "But what the heck!" She said, "I pleased them for money, you know. Money is everything. I'm thinking of my old age when I can't no longer work, when no money coming in. I need the money to hire someone to take care of me. I need the money to keep buying things that made me happy."

She went on talking and I tried to listen attentively. Although I was much tempted to tell her the instant happiness I used to have, the thrill of buying something nice to enhance my look, and the joy of having the power in possessing, I kept silent.

In fact, I also have the worries about old age and the fear of being victimized by financial institutions. I wished I could share with her my journey in search for peace of mind, but it would be a one-sided conversation. She would not hear me out anyway.

A DIFFERENT PERSON

"Today I'm a different person. I'm not me." The woman sitting next to me on a tour bus said. I turned to look at her closely. She is not her? What does she mean by that?

Catching my attention, she went on, "I have no work stress. You can't imagine how mean they are. They squeeze you like they squeeze a piece of lemon until there is no more juice and throw it away. They don't care how hard you work or how you feel. They just don't care, those store owners!" She sighed, took a deep breath and continued, "I have aches and pains all over due to bending and reaching high shelves to get the things customers want to see. The customers! Some are nice but many, many are terrible. They throw clothing on the floor, put items in the wrong racks, or hide them to wait for a sale, and change the price tags. All sorts of tricks they can think of! I constantly pick those things up and rearrange them in order. Sometimes I'm exhausted. A few minutes' break would be heavenly. But no, supervisors are watching, cameras are everywhere. But today I'm free. I have no worries, no stress. Lucky me! I was the last person to sign up for this trip. My neighbor gave me the flyer."

"I glad you came," I said.

"Me, too, I'm glad I met you, someone I can speak to in my language. I haven't spoken Vietnamese for a while. My children, their American spouses, and my grandchildren speak English only. I have no friends. I live alone. I raised my children by myself. But children, you know, they don't care what I want or how I feel. They never ask me to go on trips with them. That's why I take short trips whenever I can. Oh God! I'm old. I'm very old."

She doesn't look that old. She said earlier that she was in her seventies. She doesn't look weak, either. She is short and a bit stooped, but appears fit and alert. Her speech was clear and intelligible.

"So, why do you want to be a different person? You look fine to me." I asked.

"I've made up my mind that at least once a month I'm a different person, the one that has no anger or hatred. I'm through with hatred. My husband means nothing to me now. I despise the man who cared for his parents more than his wife and children. He chose to stay back in Vietnam to live with his parents. He did not want to go to America with us. My children then were 7, 5, and 3. I brought them up alone. Thank God! They all have good jobs."

Didn't she know how lucky she was? Her children are doing well. I guess she was lonely. I have some doubt about her husband's piety. She did mention that he loved her and their children, but why didn't he join them. There must be other reasons for his choice, remaining in Vietnam under the communist regime in spite of the fact that he was an army man of the opposite side. So thinking I asked her,

"Are you sure because of his love for his parents he chose them over you and his children?"

"He hated America and so did his parents. They don't want foreigners in their country."

"You see. Maybe that's why he did not want to come here."

"Whatever, he felt sorry for what he did to us when he was force to go to what the new regime called "Re-educational Concentration Camp," where the national officers were kept as prisoners. But it was too late. He deserved the punishment. To be honest with you I felt good. I'm now free to do what I want. At night, in my bed, I stretch my arms and legs. Nobody bothers me anymore. I just get nervous because my savings are running low, and everything is double, no, triple expensive! That's why I have to continue working. I can't wait to retire from stores. You don't know, they're mean, mean, mean!"

I feel bad for her and I really want her to enjoy the trip. I tried to distract her from her anger by calling her attention to the scenery.

"Look! Look how colorful the leaves are in this area!"

We are on our way to New Hampshire to see the foliage and to have a turkey dinner on a train ride along Winnipesaukee Lake. I put my hand on her shoulder and introduced myself, "I am Loan. What's your name?"

"Hoa. How old are you?" She asked.

"I'm also in my seventies."

"Really? You look younger. You don't have wrinkles. I feel old."

"I do, too. I can hear my bones cracking."

We laughed. Then she said, "Look at the driver! I feel sorry for him, at that age, hair all white, body like a dried tree but he still fights with the traffic and takes good care of all these elderly and disabled passengers. Life is an ocean of suffering for everyone!"

"You sound like a Buddhist." I said.

"I am. I believe there is reincarnation. In your previous lives, you were in debt with your children, your husbands, whoever. You have to pay them back during this life." She explained.

"What if we can't pay it off or we don't want to pay at all? We "quyt nợ," declare bankruptcy."

She laughed and said, "You're funny, sister. We address each other "sister," okay? This kind of debt you have to pay one life after another until you are done with it. What's the Vietnamese words you've just said? 'quyt nợ?' I like those words. Imagine that! I forget many words in my own language. No Vietnamese around to talk to.

"You don't know anybody in our community?" I asked.

"What community? There is a Vietnamese community in Boston?"

"Yes. There are lots of Vietnamese in Dorchester and thousands in Massachusetts." I said.

"I don't want to have anything to do with them. I don't like gossiping. I don't want to be bothered with jealousy and showing off. And those ex-military officers! Their glory days were long gone. And yet, the don't want to accept the fact that their war was lost. They continue to brag about their victories. I heard some of them still treat their wives like servants. I'm glad I own my life now." She paused, tapped my hand, and lowered her voice, "Nay, don't tell anybody what I said about them. They will put a communist hat on my head. The don't even bother to know why I ran away from my country. I was so afraid of the communists."

Our bus stopped at the scenic railroad Meredith Station. The group was guided to board the train by a volunteer couple. We asked them to join us at our table for four. They smiled and said they would be happy to.

Young and upbeat waiters and waitresses in their red T-shirts walked back and forth to welcome us. One said, "Real turkey, real mash potatoes, real butter squash, and real gravy. Cranberry sauce was made from scratch. Our goal at Harts Tukey Farm Restaurant will meet and exceed all of your expectation."

Everybody applauded.

"Is there such a thing as a fake turkey dinner?" Hoa asked the three of us.

"Yes, if you pay less." The wife said.

"The train started moving. The scenic ride excited us. We kept turning left and right. On one side, the lake looked peaceful spotted with white boats under the blue sky. On another, tall trees with bright red and yellow leaves lined up along the road embellished with distinguished houses here and there. We felt relaxed and happy, beginning to make acquaintance. The couple said they were originally from the Philippines. They travelled a lot, lived comfortably, and were free from family obligations. English was not a problem for them because they learned the language at early age. They had brought skills and experiences in healthcare to this country, and worked many years until they retired from their good jobs. Hoa said they were lucky, called them the privileged immigrants, and the lovebirds of the season. She asked the wife if she could borrow her husband for service on the trip. The couple encouraged her tease, cajoling her gallantly. He buttered her roll and picked up her napkins. We roared with laughter. I noticed the most serious looking passenger at another table smiled at us.

The meal finally arrived. It gave the aroma of a Thanksgiving feast. It was a real turkey dinner, warm and tasty. We cleaned up the plates. Hoa sat back, let out a long sigh and said,

"We're lucky to live in America. Today I'm really a different person. I'm free from pain and worry. I want to enjoy life. Will you all be my friends?"

AN ENCOUNTER

He has been there whenever I am at the local library. He resembles a Jesus figure with curly long hair, sad eyes, and good look. He dresses casually and seasonally. He looks clean on some days and disheveled on others. He walks up and down the stairways, stops at one bookshelf as if he were looking for some books of interest, then he moves to another, takes out a book and sits at a desk in the corner of the library. I wonder if he is really reading.

A librarian answered my questions with a smile half endearing, half amusing, "Oh! You don't know him. He makes trouble!"

"How does he make trouble?" I asked.

"He shuffles books, takes a couple of them out and places them on a different shelf."

From her I have learned that he lives in a shelter nearby. He is only allowed to stay there at night time. He comes to the library during severe weather. I often see him walking in streets. I see him standing at public areas. I want to get to know him, to talk to him, to ask him questions such as how life is in the shelter; why he ends there; and if he has a family, or how he leads his life the way he does.

I have never heard his voice and never seen him talking to anybody. There are no signs to show he enjoys anything until one day when there was a concert at the library. He tapped his fingers on the rails of the balcony to the rhythms of the music while watching a group of musicians performed on the ground floor. I was happy the whole day.

I guess he is in his fifties, no grey hair yet and upright posture. Physically, he appears intact though somewhat shaky at times. Why I am concerned about his life? Why do I want to know his personal issues? He probably does not bother to care about people's business. He is fine being himself.

I have messed the bookshelves, too. I have taken one book out, read the title, and returned it in a different order. At times I skim parts of some books and leave them on the tables. Many times, I sat at a corner of the library, reading or not. To cut down the electric bills and to be around people, I spend a lot of time out of my home. Ah! That's why I see him. Not like him, I talk when people approach me, but I seldom initiate conversations to avoid trouble or misunderstanding. I do tap to the rhythms of the music, and most of the time I am at peace being myself.

UNDERSTAND KIKI

Dogs stink. Dogs are stupid. They bark like crazy at passers-by who do nothing to them. Ignorant individuals are referred to as 'stupid like a dog.' Some of my friends and my cousin own dogs. I try to avoid being around them as much as I can because dogs are their babies and babies usually draw too much attention. There were times I felt somewhat left out as a visitor. Besides, they bother me. They scare me with their nasty grins or welcome me with their over excitement. Their paws scratch my dress or their wet tongues leave saliva on my hand. Yuck!

There is an old Vietnamese saying that goes "God is giving you what you hate." Once I was stuck in my nephew's house with Kiki, his old dog, for a week during my stay in Atlanta. When first seeing me, Kiki barked his head off until my grand-niece repeatedly yelled at him: "Kiki, stop, stop, stop, bad boy. Are you stupid or what? Go!" He looked at me suspiciously and hesitantly retreated.

My nephew and his wife left for work at five thirty every morning during my visit. They told me their work schedules were unpredictable. They both seized the opportunities to work overtime for extra pay. They gave me instructions for the day and promised a weekend trip to Helen, a German town in Georgia.

After I had walked their daughter to the bus stop I returned to let Kiki out. He darted and sniffed here and there as he was running, then stopped at a tree, lifting his leg up to urinate. Unexpectedly, he left the yard, running to a distant woody area. I guessed he had to do 'number two.' I anxiously waited for him to come back and to my delightful surprise he did. He joined me to enter the house, wandered aimlessly, stopped at the front door, looked outside through a glass window, and followed my steps as I was getting ready for cooking. The marinated chicken wings flavored with garlic and lemon grass made him restless. I felt irritated by his constantly jumpy moves asking for a treat. I gave him the only dog food he is allowed to eat and wondered how he could grow big with that kind of dried stuff. He had a long body covered with a golden fur coat and large ears. I guessed he was a shepherd breed and a knock out in his prime.

When I finally sat down in a sofa to relax, Kiki came to my side, smelled my leg and put his face on my lap. The sad and weary look in his eyes made me think of his loneliness being by himself for numerous long days. I stroke his head and gently patted his back. I found myself talking to him in silence:

"You know Kiki, I have been thinking, you and I are very much the same in that we have to depend on somebody for our needs. Right now, I really want to go sight-seeing. My nephew let me use his car but I don't know my way around and I'm afraid to drive in this big city. I'm sure you have seen those giant trucks swiftly driven on the long highways. I'm not daring anymore. Old age, you know. Sorry you got yelled at earlier. As a security guard, you tried your best to do your duty and yet you were called 'bad boy.' How were you supposed to know I was not an intruder until we really got to know each other?"

Kiki's nose was puffing as if he were glad to be understood. Encourage by his pleasing gesture I continued, "Guess what? Kiki, I was thought as being stupid, too. But I have come to realize that people don't know how smart you are unless you show them. I heard a story of a little dog being left on the beach because his owner had forgotten all about him. When she arrived home, she found him at her parking spot! I also witnessed a dog that barked at no one in a family but the woman who had kicked him several times for making a mess. I was told he continued to rebel even with the help of a psychologist. See that? You guys are smart. When we're ill-treated we have to react for our own sake, right?"

"Right! I'm glad you realized that," said Kiki by wagging his tail.

"You know something Kiki? I was even punished for doing the right thing because my ideas might hurt the interest of my boss. To some people, you're only a 'stupid' dog and I am only whatever people assume of me. That's life!"

"True," Kiki's ears stood up.

"But you and I are still lucky, Kiki," I went on, "We don't smell bad. Your owner gives you regular baths and I am still able to take care of my hygiene. I dread the day I have to rely on others for my personal care. Don't you worry, Kiki, this family is grateful to you. They told me you were their daughter's companion whenever they were unavailable. In this country animal lovers protect you, not like in some other countries where dog meat is a delicacy. Do you know why many Americans care for animals so much? Because, I guess, they need companionship and they can afford pets. Also, they want to free their offspring from the burden of tending to old parents while working and taking care of their nuclear families. On the contrary, in my country, Vietnam, the elders should be cared for by their children to show their piety. How come you're so quiet? Did my talking about piety bore you? Just one more thing Kiki, and this is between you and me: Remember, unlike children, pets are for pleasing their owners, not for causing trouble. It is much safer to know your place, okay? Oh! You are sleeping. Thanks for your company and for the opportunity to better understand you."

I saw Kiki the following year. He instantly stopped barking when he recognized me. *I've got another friend,* I thought.

THE AWAKENING MEMORY

1950. I was ten, living with my uncle's family in a mansion in a large campus. He was the superintendent of the public school a small town in South Vietnam. My uncle rescued me from being maltreated by my aunt, his younger sister who was paid by my mother to take me in during the French war. Not counting a cook and two maids, there were seven family members including me in my uncle's household: His elderly parents, his wife, and his married son, whose new bride was trying hard to win the in-laws' approval, especially her husband's demanding mother. I addressed her as 'sister Tam.' We, Vietnamese add the family rank in front of the person's name.

An incident has visited my mind now and then until today.

One early morning, sister Tam told me she wanted to meet with me at the school tennis court, where I used to wander alone listening to the singing of the birds and smelling the dews and the leaves from the surrounding trees. On that particular morning I am sure it was no different from the others, but I heard nothing and smelled nothing. I was worried. The cold look in her eyes had haunted me. The unbearable silence between us lingered for months ever since I arrived at this multi-room big house. *Am I in trouble? Why does she want to see me in private?* I tried to remember what I did to offend her. Years of experience living with my aunt I had learned to keep myself in line and to be as invisible as much as I could. I did not come up with any answers to my questions.

Here she came. Her prominent walk of a strict teacher. Her air of being in control with her big nose inflated as he was approaching closer. I shivered.

"I give you one money yesterday. I am sure you're not starving. Why did you have to eat grandma's leftover?" She asked.

I was silent, trying to remember what happened yesterday. Ah! My grandmother! The whole bowl of noodle soup was too much for her and "Wasting food is a sin." as she repeatedly reminded me. I believe feeding me was her way of showing her love and care.

"Grandma told me to finish it."

"Why didn't you tell her I gave you money for snacks? Were you starving?" She glared at me.

"I was afraid to disobey grandma," I mumbled.

"You just wanted me to look bad. That's all. Next time tell her you are not hungry because I GIVE you money every day."

She turned around and walked away. Looking at her powerful shoulders, I remembered the image of a group of her pupils grimacing behind her back in our school corridor.

A saying in Vietnamese goes as follows: "Getting away from one grave, running into another on your way out."

***

1967. During the American war my uncle moved to Saigon, where my parents resided. His family needed a temporary place to stay. We were again united under the same roof. Over the years sister Tam had proved to be a dedicated wife and a daughter-in-law. She kept the cold look but became agreeable when it came to daily talks, particularly to my mother who, by nature, went out of her way to care for her family members during wartime. My uncle's wife had no choice but to depend on her son's wife. No servants were in our house to attended to her needs.

I guess sister Tam forgot how she unfairly had treated me, and I did not bear grudges. I was an adolescent preoccupied with my first love and exciting activities in high school. However, the incident at the tennis court stayed dormant in my mind whenever there was another incident that woke it up from the coma.

1970. I was an intern in an American school learning how to teach languages. A troubled child named Angel in my class needed help from different specialists. When one of them came to get him, he immediately asked her "What time is it?" It happened that a teacher from the next class was walking by. She turned around and reprimanded the child, "Why? You want to go home now? Be quiet and go with Ms. P." Angel looked frustrated but did not say anything. Later, I asked him why he needed to know the time. He said he was afraid he would be late for counseling. Sister Tam showed up in my dream that night.

Years later I taught Vietnamese bilingual students in Boston. Some of them got punished for not understanding English or other misunderstandings. A lunch mother complained to me that Huynh was impolite. He kept walking away when she called after him several times. I found out that Huynh lost hearing aids! Sister Tam appeared visibly in my mind again!

2015. Several decades went by. My mother and sister Tam had passed away. My mother once told me sister Tam had taken good care of her when she was bed-ridden. Sister Tam's image then added a gentle smile with dimples, which I had not noticed before.

The unfair accusations have taught me the fault is not always with the child. Unpleasant memories might stay forever in my life but what to do with them is my call.

THE TWIST OF LOVE

It has been years since the last time he showed up in my dream, in which he looked like someone who was born to be admired and loved. His cape was flying in the wind as he was turning around greeting people who were looking at him in awe.

We first met when we both were seventeen years old. Thao was the tallest and best looking young man in our class. The kind look in his eyes, the broad smile, and the easy way of interacting with people won the hearts of many, especially the girls in our high school. I was one of them, but I did not realize he was my first love. In my family, romantic love was not mentioned. That kind of relationship only got approval in a marriage. Keeping that in mind, I did not show my true feelings to the opposite sex. Sensing my reserved attitude, Thao had a plan to get my attention. For months I received letters from a secret admirer named Đào. In Vietnamese 'đào' is a girl's name, for it is a name of a flower. She praised me for my writing skills and congratulated me on my role as a class leader. I wrote back to her, sharing my dreams. I dreamed big: peace on earth, poverty erased, love without borders, and the pursuit of the arts. She could not agree with me more. She had the same dreams. We finally promised to see each other after I finished performing as a leading dancer at the school year-end show. The minutes the curtain was down I anxiously left the stage and hurried to the meeting place. Thao greeted me with his famous smile and a rose in his hand. Actually, I had suspected 'the girl friend' was Thao, but I did not want to nourish my high hope.

We had our secret meetings, mostly with a group of friends or in school events. The first time he addressed me "My love" in his letter my heart beat so fast I hardly breathed. Since I looked rather pale and kept things to myself for days, my mother made me go to see a doctor!

The love thrill wore off after two years of our separation. We had different majors. He was in science and mine in Vietnamese literature.

Thao joined the drama club in his college. I had the opportunity to watch him acting with an attractive and popular girl. His letters then arrived irregularly and finally stopped completely. I knew I had lost him as a lover. In the battle with love I surrendered before competing with other girls. I did not believe I deserved his love for he was out of my reach. Not only he was a bright student, but also came from a well-to-do family. I suffered severe lovesickness. He was on my mind day and night. My thoughts and actions revolved around him. His name was deeply carved in my heart. I had the letter "T", the first letter of his name, engraved on my gold ring and pendant. I wore them for many years.

From 1954 to 1975, Vietnam was ruled by communism in the North and by nationalism in the South. Thao enthusiastically worked for the peace and the unification of the country. Whenever we happened to see each other he told me he dreamed of the day we would be together on a train that connected North and South Vietnam.

Before that day came Thao got a girl pregnant. Her parents demanded an immediate wedding. Our mutual friend informed me the news while I was studying abroad.

I moved on with my life, studying hard and working to support my family back home. By our cultural standard I was a spinster. At thirty- two years of age I was still single. Soon after I returned to my country my parents urged me to marry a persistent pursuer, whose family had a good relationship with mine. The marriage did not last long. I was widowed at thirty-eight years old. My son and I immigrated to the United States.

***

After twenty years living in Boston I received a photo of Thao embracing my mother. The sender's address was from Texas. In a trip to visit Vietnam Thao stopped by my parent's house. My mother gave him my phone number and address.

"You broke up with me without saying good bye!" That was the first line I said to him when I heard his voice saying "Hello" on the phone.

For a few second he was silent, then he explained,

"I've never meant to say good bye to you. My work for peace was dangerous. I wanted you to be safe and I intended to save your virginity for our honeymoon. Also, could not bear the thought that you would be despised by your husband in case something happened to me.

"After YOU my heart was no longer a virgin!" I retorted.

He said he did not think of virginity that way. He sincerely apologized for causing me pain.

***

Thao's wife was paralyzed by a stroke. He took good care of her, making sure to meet her needs. He used his artistic talent to entertain her by singing and telling stories. He called me to report her good and bad days. He was happy when she showed any sign of improvement. He told me he worked as a baker. He said when looking of the golden croissants he thought of the 'honey color' of my skin." He said he still remembered the drawing he did for us, in which my shining black hair and those of our imaginary daughters flowing under the moonlight. He said in darkness he would need no light since he had the image of my bright eyes. He said our love kept him going. Al the nice things he told me did not touch my hardened heart. The fire of my first love had been extinguished.

One day he cried on the phone telling me his wife had passed away. A couple of years after her funeral he came to Boston. Except for the stooped posture and the deep wrinkles on his face, the broad smile and the easy manner made my heart skip a beat or two when he appeared at the arrival gate. The man with a big heart remained, but the gentle looking in his eyes was not there. *Old age and overworked, I guess.*

He mentioned marriage. Our adult children encouraged the reunion. All my good friends were overjoyed. They offered help to take care of the wedding ceremony.

Here is a single man, the love of my early life, a chance for me to free myself from loneliness, why did I hesitate to accept his proposal?

During the week being together I found out that he had a drinking problem. He tried very hard to cover his addiction, but it showed in the ways he talked and acted. He glorified the effect of liquor and constantly craved it. He drank beer and wine days and nights. His cup of coffee smelled whiskey.

On a day trip we decided to have dinner at a restaurant. He nervously waited for a drink. When it finally came he caressed his glass of wine, held it tenderly near his heart, and brought it to his trembling lips with joy. Watching Thao treat his drink like the love of his life, I let out a long sigh. Right at that moment I knew I would never win this battle, the battle with alcoholism.

"Mr. Joe"

Five thirty in the morning I arrived at the YMCA pool in Quincy. Some of the familiar faces looked surprised because I was earlier than usual. Mary and I often share the same lane. At eight-two she is a regular. Our chats are mostly checking on our health. "Did you have trouble sleeping?" She asked. "No," I answered. "On the contrary, I had a great time yesterday and a restful night." Mary raised her eyebrows waiting for me to say more.

"I attended a Memorial Service for a man known as "Mr. Joe." I had never met him, just heard about his good deeds. He passed away weeks ago but the service was held yesterday in New Hampshire."

"You drove that far by yourself?" Mary asked.

"No, I joined a group of acquaintances. They all do volunteering work at the Vietnamese community in the Boston area. I am a newcomer. Seven of us are different in age and profession but that day we had the same thought in mind: Paying respect to a noble soul. You wouldn't believe what he did, Mary. In order to bring hundreds of Vietnamese children with polio and burn victims to this country for treatment he had to sell his house after he exhausted his savings and credit cards! And you know what his last act was? He offered his body to Harvard University for research."

"God blessed his soul! I'm telling you, he is a saint, an image of Jesus." Mary exclaimed.

Then she started retelling the miracle stories of her faith that cured her illness and saved her troubled children. I listened with curiosity but did not say anything because I do not have much knowledge of any religion and also lose trust in those who claim themselves 'religious people.' But Mr. Joe was different. I wondered if he would have done such great things if he were not a Christian. All day long I kept thinking of the power of belief that has helped people with less suffering and become more forgiving. Also, the scene of the service repeatedly played over in my mind.

More than two hundred guests including Mr. Joe's adopted Vietnamese children and their friends were present. The sound of our hymn singing brought the feelings of warmth and closeness among us.

One by one some guests came up to the stage to share their appreciation of Mr. Joe's kindness and his generous contribution to the disadvantaged.

We learned from his friends that he went out of his way to deal with the complicated policies of both countries to bring these disabled children to the United States. He treated them as his own, continuously providing them with food, shelter, medication, and therapy. Being diagnosed with polio at an early age, Mr. Joe had much sympathy for the children under his care. Therefore, he made sure thy had a good education. "No excuse for ignorance was his motto.

Mr. Joe's friend. A minister. Believes whoever loves Christ has much love for mankind. Faith is the gift that the Lord placed in Mr. Joe's heart. Love brings people together. "The world needs to hear the word "God." He repeated what Mr. Joe often said.

After a roaring applause, a Caucasian said that Mr. Joe gave him a chance to have a Vietnamese daughter. The girl was a burn victim who is now a happy married woman, and "she calls me DAD!"

Next was a Vietnamese man expressing his admiration to Mr. Joe, an American who deeply cared for the children from a foreign country. He hoped the wealthy Vietnamese-Americans would not forget the poor and the sick.

It has been a long time since I cried, but tears streaked down my face when the sight of a Vietnamese young man wearing an amiable smile dragging his weak leg caused by polio appeared from the crowd to give thanks to the attendees. In his perfect English, he introduced himself as Tuan Nguyen, the heir of Mr. Joe. He said, "Everything I am and I have now I owe to Mr. Joe. I will follow his steps. I'll continue his quest of charity." Then he invited us to enjoy the meal prepared by Mr. Joe's Vietnamese children and friends.

Our group had a great time making friends and savoring delicious homemade Vietnamese dishes.

On our way home we were more relaxed and open, sharing our work experience, wishes, and nostalgia. We miss our homeland and we are eager to make it a better place by providing financial aid to our countrymen. Here, in America, we try to do what we can to care for the Vietnamese-American children. The three professional young mothers who volunteer teaching Vietnamese on weekends left their children home with their husbands to join the group. At times, they interrupted the on-going conversations to talk with their children on the phone, reminding them to do their homework. The driver, a volunteer administrator, has devoted many years supporting the Vietnamese community. His attractive and efficient wife taught us how to prepare authentic Vietnamese food. Being new in this country she wanted to linger the moments of being with the native Vietnamese speakers at the social gatherings. The electrician, who was married twice, now lives with his friends. He boasted he could fix most everything without knowing much English. Then he grinned, showing spaces between his front teeth, which he didn't seem to care.

"Love feeds love and hate feeds hate." This line suddenly ran through my mind. Mr. Joe's love for people has been widely spread. It was his death that brought us together. I, an accidental passenger, have eventually received the care and love from my new friends.

When coming home I called those who knew Mr. Joe to learn more of his life. One of his friends told me to read about him online. I clicked on the title "Child Medical Connection" and Joseph B. Bodanza photos appeared on YouTube. He looked kind and elegant next to the faces of the bewildered Vietnamese children at an airport. Other pictures showed children with deformed features. The speaker, John Brown, reported that Mr. Joe was a retired high school teacher. Convinced by a Vietnamese friend, he reluctantly made a trip to Vietnam. He was amazed by the natural beauty of this country and felt compelled to do something for the children whose twisted spines and legs were regarded as a curse to their families. He volunteered to make the following trips and since then those miserable lives have been changed from "the way they look to how they think" as Tuan once said.

A Boston Globe journalist, Sam Allis, noted the followings:

"Sixty-eight years old, Joe Bodanza went to Vietnam for the first time in 1996. Two years later he established the non-profit "Child Medical Connection Inc." He received donation but managed the organization on his own." For more than 15 years he worked hard through several strokes and a bout of cancer to provided financial support to the needy children who have lived in this country and in Vietnam."

A close friend of Mr. Joe told me over the phone, "Giving is receiving. I think Joe did not mean to receive favor but he had gained so much love and gratitude from those who knew him. "Mr. Joe" went to the other world leaving us an everlasting spiritual gift. It should be shared with many others."

A FAIRY TALE

Once upon a time there were two kingdoms separated by an ocean. One was called Niceland and the other Fineland.

People in Niceland toiled rice fields and raised animal. These peasants and farmers enjoyed the natural resources of their small country. Under the tropical sun, flowers and fruit trees were abundant. Rivers and waterfalls refreshed their souls. Although they were quite content with their simple lives, they wished to have enough food and clothing, and especially, schools for their children.

On the contrary, people in Fineland lived comfortably in all seasons. Numerous ones enjoyed luxurious life styles with plenty of delicious food and fancy clothing for each season. Schools and hospitals were built everywhere on this vast land. It was said that by law even the sick and the poor were protected. Many people from others countries risked their lives to come to Fineland to find safety and comfort.

In Niceland lived a pretty girl named Maleen. Her parents owned a small store. Maleen helped by serving their customers. Whoever had come to know Maleen would have praised her for her kindness, her shining black hair, sparkling eyes, and bright smile. Maleen and Sunno were lovers. The young man was full of vigor and love for his people. He wanted to become a soldier to protect his country, which for decades had been invaded by powerful rulers. While he was away for military training Maleen had a number of suitors. The news reached Sunno. He thought Maleen betrayed him. He immediately left his post and hurried home to find out the truth. Upon arrival he saw Maleen smile when talking to a customer who resembled a foreign enemy. Sunno's blood was boiling with jealousy and hatred. He planned to hurt Maleen badly, thinking without her pretty face no man would want her. One night, he came out of a leafy tree and splashed acid on her face while she was walking home from work. Maleen's beauty was destroyed and her belief in mankind shattered. She wanted to disappear forever.

A wealthy couple from Fineland heard about Maleen's tragedy. They offered to bring her to their country, where they hoped she would be helped by well-trained healers to restore her appearance.

Under the hands of the skillful medicine men, Maleen's face looked less grotesque. However, she continued to cover her face with a scarf wherever she went. She dreaded to see the scrutinized and repulsive looks of those she encountered.

One day when Maleen was waiting for her turn to receive treatment, a middle age woman with a disfigured face introduced herself as Lenia and started a conversation with Maleen. They exchanged their stories and later became friends. Maleen learned that Lenia, a burn victim grew up in Fineland, where all citizens, at their early ages, were taught to respect differences among people. She advised Maleen to go bare face. She said, "in this land people respect you as a person in spite of your misfortune."

"But I'm afraid they will make fun of me, stare at me, or avoid me like some people did to me back home," Maleen responded.

"Don't you worry about their poor manners. If they do so, ignore them. Remember you have a right to be on earth just like everyone else. Keep smiling and protect your mind, you will be alright. It's your face that was deformed, not your brain, nor your heart."

Maleen listened to her friend. She practiced showing her real face and worked hard to become a nurse.

A young apprentice of medicine admired Maleen for her courage and determination to improve her overall well-being. He was in love with her. His friends called him 'Grant the Great' for the good deeds he had done.

Maleen could not believe her ears when Grant Zeno asked her to be his wife. Although she thought very highly of Grant and contemplated his handsome features, she could not dream of having a wonderful man like Grant. She accepted his proposal with much doubt and worry. She wondered if Grant asked for her hand out of pity and if his family would accept her as a daughter-in-law?

It turned out that Grant's parents trusted their son's choice. They treated Maleen as their own daughter.

Together Maleen and Grant made a great couple. They built their own house and warmed their home with friends and relatives. Their lovely children completed their dream. Maleen did not forget Sunno's life in prison. She sent a letter to the judge in her hometown asking him to set Sunno free. Also, she wrote a note to Lenia as follows:

"Dear Lenia, thanks to your advice and encouragement I have tried my best to rebuild myself and now my life is full of joy. One person hurt me but many others saved me. You are one of them. Thank you so very much. Lenia. Your devoted friend. Maleen."

The Maleen-Grant Zeno family lived happily ever after.

NAMING

My name is *Trần Thị Kim Lan*. It's a Vietnamese name. *Trần* is my family name and *Lan* is my given name. *Thi* indicates a female gender and *Kim* (gold) goes with *Lan* (orchid) meaning *Golden Orchid*. Most Vietnamese names carry wishes of parents. Common names for women symbolize different kinds of flowers, virtues, precious stones, ..., while men's names usually characterize courage, success, power, and many others that sound smart and heroic.

Our national language called "*quốc ngữ*" uses Roman alphabet. This phonetic script was primarily devised by a French Jesuit priest and a linguist, Alexandre de Rhode, to preach his faith. My name, thus is written with alphabet and a few tonal marks. We stopped using Chinese characters in the early 1900s.

In America, first name goes first and last name goes last. My name now is *Lan Tran* or *Kim Lan Tran*.

I also got more than one name along the way since I was a little girl. I used to laugh easily and to smile a lot. It was just me. I did not choose to be that way. But some of my cousins thought it was ridiculous to show my white teeth, which was in contrast with my skin color. They named me "Mười Đười Ươi," meaning "Ape Tenth." That was to say I grinned like an ape. Ha! Ha! They were amused by the three last rhythmic letters of each word "ươi." *Mười* (ten) is my other name addressed in my

135

family. I have twelve siblings. Birth order is commonly used as first name.

My complexion is light brown like my mother's. Some of my brothers and sisters have my father's fair skin. Many Vietnamese including my family members favor fair or white skin, which is usually not left out when describing a beautiful woman. The opposite of 'white' is 'black' and 'black to them means 'ugly.' I was then called "Black Ten" (Mười Đen)

Years later when I returned home from America with a bachelor degree, my uncle, an educator, was overjoyed. He called me "White Ten." (Mười Trắng) *Ah! Education made me white!*

Thinking back, those name callings did not really bother me much. Either I had good nature or was too naive to feel humiliated. However, I wondered why I was the target of being ridiculed. I look at my old photo and was surprised that my skin color or a 'defect' to some people was more noticeable than my lustrous long hair, bright eyes, full lips, and fine skin. Luckily, a few lines from one of my suitors in my prime saved my pride. He wrote:

> *Honey, the color of your skin*
> *Light, the look in your eyes*
> *Stream, the flow of your hair*
> *They are meant for me to share*
> *Oh! I love, love you so much, my love.*

Here comes the fun thing. One of my American bosses thought Asian women did not drink and she knew I rarely touched liquor. At a New Year party, she told me to "cheer" with her. I did so to please her and to go along with the happy crowd. She was all excited, immediately named me "Kim Lan Blast." It turned out I liked the name "Blast." I wanted to blast. I was tired of being submissive and obedient, of ignoring insults and bulling.

I found myself rebelling like an adolescent. Forget about *Golden Orchid!* It sounds like one of the names of a character in cheap romantic novels. Besides, I did not see myself as a flower, too weak to survive the on-going wars in Vietnam and the hard life as an immigrant with constant adjustment to multi-cultures in the new country. I'm different now. I have tried to give myself a name in accordance to the qualities I wish I had more, from *Nhân Ái* (compassion), or *Tương Ái* (love one another) to some memorable places as *Cà Mau,* where I was born, or *U Minh,* the mosquitos' terrain, where my brother and I were starved for days, trying to escape from the attacks of these hungry creatures by dipping our bodies in the river. Hearing the shooting nearby our hired boatman had run for his life leaving us on a boat with little food.

I really like the name *U Minh,* not because the hardship we undertook, but also because *U* means 'dark' and *Minh* means 'bright.' *U Minh* fits my knowledge about life. Darkness and brightness are the creations of God(s) whether we want to accept them or not.

As I grew older, I understood my parents better and especially their wishes. They wished me to be a lasting flower by adding the word '*Kim*' as my middle name. They might want me to live truly to my gender, performing well the role of a woman, who is caring for others and devoted to her family, but always gentle and delicate as a flower. "Jeez! That's hard!" My students would exclaim hearing this. Or they just did what they had learned from their ancestors who adopted Confucius' teaching. Whatever their wishes were I'd like to show respect and gratitude to them for their best intention. I decided to keep the original name. I stopped dwelling on names that mean nothing but labeling, and labels do not reflect my true self.

A very dear lady I called Mom who treated me like her own daughter, my good friend from college. Mom used to check on her adult children and me to see if we were home from work during severe weather. Over the phone she asked me, "Are you home, Ann?" Ann is her daughter-in-law. I corrected her, "Mom, I'm Lan." She retorted, "Whatever your name is, are you home safely? You know who I'm talking to."

After I hung up the phone I said to myself, "If nothing else, my parents and my American mother wished for me were to be safe and to really know who I am."

ABOUT THE AUTHOR

Kim Lan Tran, the author of "Gió Đêm" (Night Wind) written in Vietnamese, and "Tết: The New Year" was born in Vietnam and received higher education in the United States. A long-time resident of Massachusetts, she has worked as a school psychologist and a language teacher.